Public Reading of
Scripture

Public Reading of Scripture

Scripture

A HANDBOOK

Clayton J. Schmit

ABINGDON PRESS
Nashville

PUBLIC READING OF SCRIPTURE
A HANDBOOK

Copyright © 2002 by Abingdon Press

This book is printed on acid-free, recycled, elemental-chlorine–free paper.

Library of Congress Cataloging-in-Publication Data

Schmit, Clayton J.
    Public reading of scripture: a handbook / Clayton J Schmit.
        p.   cm.
Includes bibliographical references.
    ISBN 0-687-04537-1
1. Bible—Reading.   2. Reading in public worship. I. Title.
BS617 .S265 2002
264'.34—dc21

2001006906

Scripture quotations are from the New Revised Standard Version of the Bible, copyright © 1989, by the Division of Christian Education of the National Council of the Churches of Christ in the United States of America. Used by permission.

The quotation from St. Augustine's *Homilies on the Gospel of John*, in chapter 2, is taken from *The Nicene and Post-Nicene Fathers of the Christian Church*, vol. 7, ed. Philip Schaff (Grand Rapids: Eerdmans, 1956).

In chapter 2, page 35, the Karl Barth quotation is taken from *Homiletics*, trans. Geoffrey W. Bromiley and Donald E. Daniels (Louisville, KY: Westminster/John Knox Press, 1991), p. 78.

The chapter 3 epigraph is taken from Saint Bonaventure, *Collations on the Six Days*, *Thirteenth Collation*, in *The Works of Bonaventure*, vol. 5, trans. José de Vinck (Paterson, N.J.: St. Anthony Guild Press, 1970).

The chapter 5 epigraph is taken from John Calvin, *Institutes of the Christian Religion*, trans. John Allen (Philadelphia: Presbyterian Board of Christian Education, n.d. [1813], vol. 1, bk. 3, 33-36, pp. 636-40, as quoted in Richard Lischer, *Theories of Preaching: Selected Readings in the Homiletical Tradition* (Durham, N.C.: The Labyrinth Press, 1987).

In chapter 5, the quotation from Martin Luther is taken from *Luther's Works: Table Talk*, vol. 54, ed. and trans. Theodore G. Tappert (Philadelphia: Fortress Press, 1967).

02 03 04 05 06 07 08 09 10—10 9 8 7 6 5 4 3 2 1

MANUFACTURED IN THE UNITED STATES OF AMERICA

To Gene & Marcy Schmit,
who first placed in my hands the
Holy Scriptures

Contents

Introduction

> Then the king [Josiah] directed that all the elders of Judah and Jerusalem should be gathered to him. The king went up to the house of the LORD, and with him went all the people of Judah, all the inhabitants of Jerusalem, the priests, the prophets, and all the people, both small and great; he read in their hearing all the words of the book of the covenant that had been found in the house of the LORD.
>
> —2 Kings 23:1-2

Since the days of Luther's translation of the Bible into the vernacular and the use of Gutenberg's press to disseminate it, the Scriptures have been in use in the hands of Christian laypeople. But their significance for the life and worship of God's people predate that by many hundreds of years. When the high priest Hilkiah found the book of the law hidden in the Temple in Jerusalem, King Josiah read it aloud himself before all the people. He was, it seems, the first layperson to read the written word of God aloud in public worship. Today, the practice is common. But a person's willingness to serve as a reader in worship does not necessarily correlate with an ability to do this well. The purpose of this book is twofold: (1) to provide Christian laymen and laywomen with an understanding of the importance of serving as readers of Scripture in public worship, and (2) to serve as a resource in teaching them to perform this ministry effectively. The audience for this volume is principally those persons who feel called to undertake this form of proclamation in their congregations. While this book may find some use in seminaries as a resource for teaching future pastors the skills of public reading and interpretation of Scripture, it is designed primarily for laypeople. It is intended as a practical volume that will deal with issues relating to the use of body, voice, and mind in making the Scriptures come alive in public reading. Along the way, certain theological issues, such as the discernment of call and consideration of public Scripture reading as a form of proclamation, will be discussed. But the central thrust of this book is to assist laypeople in becoming effective readers in their congregations.

This book has been prepared under the assumption that the best way to learn about reading Scripture in public is in a small-group classroom setting. Though the book can be used by individuals, the hope is that congregations will establish a team of teachers who will offer classes on Scripture reading for worship. The discussion questions and exercises interspersed throughout this text are especially geared for such small group or classroom use.

The public reading of Scripture is a mode of oral interpretation of literature. This aspect of speech communication is also known as dramatic reading and is taught in courses at many universities. Oral interpretation is an art that employs techniques for body and voice to make written texts come alive as they are spoken. In secular settings, the art is applied to the reading of poetry and story. Our task here is to demonstrate how these techniques can also be used to bring life to the reading of scriptural texts in worship.

Many churches have much to learn about oral interpretation of Scripture. My own pastoral training was at a Lutheran seminary where the topic of oral interpretation of Scripture was not raised a single time in the four years I was a student there. Today, in a growing number of seminaries, courses in the oral interpretation of Scripture are being offered. They are typically taught by teachers of preaching or worship. Still, in some schools a course like this has never been taught. One seminary that has taken this ministry seriously over the years is Princeton Theological Seminary. Those who visit its campus in New Jersey will find not just a classroom or teacher devoted to speech communication and oral interpretation of Scripture, but a speech communication building and numerous offices, classrooms, and speech laboratories dedicated to teaching these practical matters. It is no wonder, then, that some of the best written resources on the subject have been authored by those who teach (or were taught) these things at Princeton. The annotated bibliography in the appendix section of this volume will point the reader to some of these resources as well as others that might be considered for further study and training. The material provided in this book is intended as a starting point for those laypeople who want to consider carefully the invitation to become involved in this type of ministry.

Because this book is intended principally for laypeople, most technical language will be avoided as we discuss this ministry. However, let me offer one liturgical term that can serve us well as a synonym for the more awkward phrase "reader of Scripture in public worship." The word is *lector* and refers to a person who reads from an appointed passage of Scripture. A small set of related terms may also be useful to define. An appointed Scripture reading is known as a *lection* and comes from a collection known as a *lectionary*. Often the lector reads from a podium that is known as a *lectern*.

As we proceed, two other terms will be kept before us: *talent* and *skill*. It will be helpful at the outset to define these terms as they are used in this text. *Talent* refers to the natural capacity that an individual has for performing particular tasks. Most people have a little talent for many things. Not everyone can draw beautifully, but most can draw well enough to play the games "Hangman" or "Pictionary." Those who wish to draw better can learn to do so through classes and study. But some people are given the natural capacity and receptivity to learn the techniques that will make them exceptional artists. They are not born great artists, but they are born with an innate ability and potential for artistic expression. Talent is a gift, bestowed by our Creator. Whether talent is used, developed, and fulfilled is a personal choice. Yet the original capacity is simply God's gift.

Skill refers to the techniques employed in the accomplishment of a task. Whether or not one is especially talented in a particular area, he or she can acquire certain skills related to it. Playing the guitar involves the techniques of strumming, fingering, and music reading. Those who have special talent for this activity will acquire the skills more readily and accomplish more with them than a person with average talent. This means that certain levels of skill can be acquired by any interested student. Yet those with talent will find less frustration and more fulfillment in the utilization of skills that are acquired readily and employed fruitfully. It seems to be a law of nature that people most enjoy doing those things for which they have the most talent. Or, to put it in scriptural terms, it seems to be true that people enjoy performing ministry tasks for which they have particular spiritual gifts. As we proceed, we will consider how talent and skill are related to spiritual gifts. We will also discuss which gifts and skills are most useful for those who undertake the ministry of public Scripture reading.

Such matters will be taken up in the first chapter, the purpose of which will be to assist people in assessing their call to serve in the ministry of reading Scripture in worship. The second chapter will focus on oral interpretation of Scripture as an important form of biblical proclamation. In the third chapter, we will consider issues having to do with studying God's word in preparation for delivering it orally. Chapters 4 and 5 represent the heart of this project. They deal with specific techniques and offer suggestions and opportunities for practice in becoming an effective lector. The focus of chapter 4 is on use of the body in bringing Scripture readings to life. Chapter 5 will consider the use of oral interpretation techniques. As mentioned above, each chapter contains questions for group discussion and exercises, designed to guide the readers' practice in preparing for oral interpretation of Scripture. Chapters 1, 2, and 3 each *conclude* with discussion questions and a few exercises to get trainees warmed up for public Scripture reading. In the final chapters, the discussion of each topic is followed immediately by pertinent exercises. The intent is that the learner first practice the exercises while studying in private and then perform them in the small group setting in order to receive feedback from the group's instructor and members. The book's end material includes two appendixes. Appendix A offers a list of suggested approaches for creative Scripture reading in worship. In order to point the reader and student in the direction of further resources for continuing education, an annotated bibliography is included as appendix B. It provides commentary on several useful books and video resources that can help readers continue to grow in their technique.

I wish to thank several people who have assisted me in the creation of this project. First, I am grateful to my colleagues in the Performance Studies Group of the Academy of Homiletics, especially Charles Bartow, Jana Childers, and Richard Ward, who continue to teach me what it means to bring the Scriptures to life in oral presentation. I am also grateful to Pastor Bill Crabtree for his initial insight about the need to address this topic. Additionally, I am eager to thank a number of laypeople who are committed to the ministry of reading Scripture in worship. They have given me encouragement, frank and useful feedback, and the chance to learn from their work as successful lectors. They are Shelly McCormick Westby, Michael Evans, Brian Tolson, Brede Westby, Marilyn Lee, and Stewart Fries. Finally, I thank God for the constant love, support, and companionship of my attorney, Carol Vallely Schmit.

Chapter 1

HOW BEAUTIFUL THE FEET

How beautiful upon the mountains are the feet of the messenger who announces peace, who brings good news, who announces salvation, who says to Zion, "Your God reigns." Listen! Your sentinels lift up their voices, together they sing for joy; for in plain sight they see the return of the LORD to Zion. Break forth together into singing, you ruins of Jerusalem; for the LORD has comforted his people, he has redeemed Jerusalem. The LORD has bared his holy arm before the eyes of all the nations; and all the ends of the earth shall see the salvation of our God.

—Isaiah 52:7-10

How beautiful are the feet, the voice, the presence of those who dare to proclaim the Word of the Lord. For they are bearers of a word that is filled with promise, hope, encouragement, correction, and good news. God's Word is as much needed in our day as in any. People are searching for truth while the statements of public officials are being parsed and probed for meaning. People are seeking spiritual fulfillment through gimmicky literature and vaguely spiritual mountain retreats. Children are looking for limits in a new world that defies definition and questions all previous modes of knowing. As Christians, we believe that the Word of God is timeless and relevant to the restlessness of people today. Even more, we believe that in God's Word lie the answers to the most pressing questions of human inquiry. The Bible gives us guidance for life and reveals God's promises in Jesus Christ. He alone, the one whom John calls the Living Water, can most deeply quench the thirst of those whose souls long for refreshment.

There is no more important proclamation, today or in any age, than the public speaking of the Word of God. Chiefly, we proclaim this message in public worship as God speaks to us through the Scriptures. Preachers use the Word as the basis for their sermons, messages that are prepared to draw a connection between the affairs of people's lives and God's word of promise. But before the proclamation of preaching is the proclamation of reading God's Word aloud. When the Word is read, God's people hear it and are transformed by it. Those who rise, stand in the midst of their peers, and proclaim God's Word are beautiful, in Isaiah's sense of the word.

Isaiah spoke of the herald, the fleet-footed messenger whose duty was to run swiftly to the anxious people of the city to deliver news of a battle or to announce the arrival of a king. The herald's beauty lay in the swiftness of his feet, the means of delivery. The herald of today is also bringing a needed word to an expectant people. We choose heralds for reading Scripture in public worship not by the swiftness of their feet, but for their ability to present themselves gracefully and to render the readings intelligibly. They are beautiful not in any traditional aesthetic sense, but in the sense that they skillfully bring what is needed—good news from the God who made us and who continues to care for us. Their presence, their skill, their thoughtful articulation of God's Word: these are the things that are beautiful.

As a child, I was given the annual task of assisting my grandmother in preparing the Christmas turkey. Each Christmas Eve my sister and I would go to her house and spend several hours setting the table, chopping the vegetables, and grinding the mysterious rubbery meats that would go in the dressing. The preparation, of course, was not pretty. It was painstaking: getting things just the way Grandma liked them, pulling the heart and giblets from the cavity where they once served vital life functions, trying to cut them into chunks as they squirted away beneath the knife's edge. But the preparation was necessary for the feast. At the appointed hour on Christmas Day, after the entire family had arrived, Grandma would present the fruits of our labors. She would bring the bird forth, stuffed and cooked, brown and steaming, moist and fragrant. These things were beautiful: the smell of the food, the kitchen's warmth emanating through an open door, the anticipation and joy of the family, the look of satisfaction on Grandma's face, and a meal well prepared and fittingly delivered to a hungry and expectant people. In the same way, how beautiful is the presentation of readers who do well in bringing forth God's Word to a hungry and expectant people, making the written word come alive, filling people's imaginations with sights, smells, sounds, and scenes that echo life.

WHOSE JOB IS IT TO READ THE SCRIPTURES IN WORSHIP?

Increasingly, churches are coming to see the value of involving laypeople in the leadership of public worship. Not long ago the chancel was strictly the province of pastor or priest. But the doctrine of the priesthood of all believers, and an increasing awareness of the range of spiritual gifts that God brings to each assembly, have changed things. One of the focuses of liturgical renewal in the past few decades has been to return to the sense that worship is a holy activity that involves us all. It is not just something performed by the professionals on behalf of the untutored. This shift has allowed the clergy to step aside so that the various ministries of worship leadership can be shared by capable and gifted laypeople. When this happens, the clergy's role shifts. No longer the solitary leaders of worship, they take the lead in finding ways to provide training for laypersons who wish to serve in worship roles. As the trained professionals in matters of prayer leadership, chanting, or Scripture reading, the clergy undertake to equip the saints for performing these functions. If they are sufficiently expert in these roles, the clergy may teach these skills themselves. If not, they may seek help in training laypeople to be effective worship leaders. They may also need assistance in knowing how to select the proper people for involvement in such important public ministries.

When a congregation is committed to the involvement of laypeople in worship leadership, problems may occur if insufficient preparation has been provided for these roles. In some settings, the following scene is all too frequently enacted:

Just as a service of worship is about to begin, an usher informs the pastor that the person appointed for reading the Scripture lessons that morning has called in sick. Quickly, the pastor scans the assembly and finds a likely replacement. "Let's get Janet to do it," she says. "She's not afraid of speaking in public." Hurriedly, the usher rushes off to inform Janet of her new duty and sends her to the pastor for hasty instructions.

Should Janet accept this last-minute appointment? The urgency of the moment might compel her to do so. Yet, if she were to consider the matter carefully, she might choose to decline. The public reading of Scripture is an important part of worship and ought to be performed with careful preparation. Reading well in worship involves certain skills that take time to acquire and polish, just as in playing an organ prelude, preaching a sermon, or ushering people effectively during the distribution of Holy Communion. If the pastor were told that the *preacher* for the morning had called in sick and that she needed suddenly to fill in for him, she would be at a complete loss. Even if she could deliver the same sermon the preacher had written and had his full sermon text to use, she would want to have the opportunity to read it through several times, practice speaking it aloud, and work at finding the right emphases and gestures to match the sermon's logic and flow. If Janet were inclined to accept the invitation to read the Scriptures in worship, it would not be less appropriate for her to expect time to prepare the reading. Also, beyond having the chance to prepare well, there are other considerations. Does Janet have a suitable voice? Is there a public address system, and is she familiar with its use? Does Janet have sufficient biblical knowledge, and does she know the background of the particular lessons she is being asked to read? Does Janet have the confidence to stand before the assembly and speak God's Word? Can she interpret the text in a meaningful way? Can Janet read so as to bring life to the reading and unfold its meaning to her listeners? That is a lot for Janet to consider in the moment. Her answer to these questions might lead her to decline the invitation on this occasion and to avoid participating in this type of ministry altogether. For, clearly, such a responsibility is not for everyone. Reading Scriptures as a public ministry, whether you are lay or ordained, requires certain skills, suitable training, some particular spiritual gifts, and a sense of call.

CALLED TO SERVE

What does it mean to be called to serve in such a capacity? Does the call to lay ministries come simply from the voice of the pastor who looks out over the congregation, hoping to spot willing souls to fill various roles? Does it come through the system of congregational committees whereby a duly appointed chairperson calls on people to serve? Or, does it come, in any sense, from God? Paul is helpful here. He tells us in several writings that the call to serve the church has to do with the spiritual gifts with which God empowers the body of Christ. Here is his explanation of these things as delivered to the troubled church in Corinth:

> Now concerning spiritual gifts, brothers and sisters, I do not want you to be uninformed. . . .
> Now there are varieties of gifts, but the same Spirit; and there

are varieties of services, but the same Lord; and there are varieties of activities, but it is the same God who activates all of them in everyone. To each is given the manifestation of the Spirit for the common good. To one is given through the Spirit the utterance of wisdom, and to another the utterance of knowledge according to the same Spirit, to another faith by the same Spirit, to another gifts of healing by the one Spirit, to another the working of miracles, to another prophecy, to another the discernment of spirits, to another various kinds of tongues, to another the interpretation of tongues. All these are activated by one and the same Spirit, who allots to each one individually just as the Spirit chooses.

For just as the body is one and has many members, and all the members of the body, though many, are one body, so it is with Christ. For in the one Spirit we were all baptized into one body— Jews or Greeks, slaves or free—and we were all made to drink of one Spirit.

Indeed, the body does not consist of one member but of many. If the foot would say, "Because I am not a hand, I do not belong to the body," that would not make it any less a part of the body. And if the ear would say, "Because I am not an eye, I do not belong to the body," that would not make it any less a part of the body. If the whole body were an eye, where would the hearing be? If the whole body were hearing, where would the sense of smell be? But as it is, God arranged the members in the body, each one of them, as he chose. . . .

Now you are the body of Christ and individually members of it. And God has appointed in the church first apostles, second prophets, third teachers; then deeds of power, then gifts of healing, forms of assistance, forms of leadership, various kinds of tongues. Are all apostles? Are all prophets? Are all teachers? Do all work miracles? Do all possess gifts of healing? Do all speak in tongues? Do all interpret? But strive for the greater gifts.

(1 Corinthians 12:1, 4-18, 27-31a)

The body of Christ, as manifested in the local congregation, has many services to perform. As members of it, we are to go into the world proclaiming Christ and performing as his servants in various ways. We also have the duty to see to the maintenance of the congregation, its buildings, the people's welfare, and especially the care of their souls. The pastor cannot do all of this. The pastor is a leader who trains, encourages, and sometimes admonishes the congregation in order to see to these ministries. He or she is also a well-trained and spiritually gifted individual who can interpret God's Word for the congregation and lead in varieties of teaching, counseling, visitation, and worship ministries. But, as Paul assures us, *all* members of the body of Christ have spiritual gifts. They are given according to God's good pleasure and are to be used for the well-being of the church. God provides the human resources, endows us with spiritual gifts, and activates them according to God's needs. If we are to serve Christ, then we serve at God's pleasure and appointment. If we are to serve effectively, we do so by putting to use those gifts that God has given us.

Sometimes the call to serve becomes misdirected. Paul reminds us that the eye cannot function as well as an ear. Why, then, do congregations so often recruit people to serve in positions for which they are not gifted? Why do we presume that a person gifted for teaching children should make critical decisions about boiler replacement or parking lot pavement? Undiscriminating devotion to the idea that the ministry of the church belongs to all the people leads us to seek willing people to serve in available positions without regard for their talents and inclinations. Often it does more harm than good. Recruiting willing servants to perform in roles for which they are not gifted fosters burnout among a congregation's volunteers. People once eager to serve Christ may find their service unfulfilling and unsatisfactory. There is little joy in performing a task for which one is not qualified. Yet people continue to serve out of a sense of Christian duty, finding perhaps some satisfaction in knowing that such service is a form of cross bearing. There are, however, many who serve in their congregation's ministry both successfully and joyfully. They are the ones who serve in areas for which they have particular talents.

Does talent have anything to do with one's spiritual gifts? Clearly, Paul indicates that it does. God appoints and activates people according to their gifts. These gifts are not instant charisms that come in the moment of baptism. Adults who are baptized are not miraculously enabled to perform new duties. Musical talents or the ability to preach do not descend instantaneously on a person like a dove. Our talents are part of who God made each individual to be. The psalmist beautifully reminds us that we are fashioned and known, even from our mother's womb:

> For it was you who formed my inward parts;
>   you knit me together in my mother's womb.
> I praise you, for I am fearfully and wonderfully made.
>   Wonderful are your works;
> that I know very well.
>   My frame was not hidden from you,
> when I was being made in secret,
>   intricately woven in the depths of the earth.
> Your eyes beheld my unformed substance.
> In your book were written
> all the days that were formed for me,
>   when none of them as yet existed.
>   (Psalm 139:13-15)

God makes us, endows us with talents, and brings them to spiritual use through our baptism into Christ. In the book of Acts we see that Saul's talents for administration of an anti-Christian crusade became Paul's spiritual gifts for the building of the church. His brilliance as a scholar and theological inquirer became the foundation for his work as a shaper of Christian doctrine and thought. His gifts for classical rhetoric were the genesis for his calling as an apostle and preacher of the gospel of Christ. In the same way, we are naturally gifted and, because we are members of the body of Christ, God puts those gifts to work in spiritual ways. The call to serve in ministry, whether as a layperson or as a member of the clergy, is related directly to a person's talents and to God's will as God chooses to use personal endowments for the good of the church.

Does inclination have anything to do with one's sense of call? In many ways, it does. People usually enjoy doing things they are good at. Great dancers love to dance. Singers cannot cease from singing. Poets write because they are bursting to give expression to the mysteries of life. Composers wander through life with music constantly filling their heads. Our talents are natural elements of how we have been fearfully and wonderfully made. They please us as well as give us direction. A child good in math finds that engineering is an enjoyable field of study. An athlete of great size finds joy in the crush of the football scrimmage line. A person equally gifted in scientific inquiry and compassion finds nursing to be a natural manifestation of his or her personhood. Yet our perceptions of who we are and what we enjoy are often clouded by circumstance. We may not know that we possess a talent, because we have not had the opportunity to try our hand at a task. We may have had a sour experience that makes us fearful to undertake something that might otherwise delight us. There is a natural fear associated with performance-related endeavors because they place us in front of people who will judge us. And, if we have insufficient training, even high degrees of talent may go undeveloped and be of little use. I have a friend who grew to dislike piano lessons as a child because his mother was the local piano teacher and he was constantly pressured by her to play. Around age nine, he became bold enough to ask how long he had to take piano lessons. "You can quit taking lessons as soon as you can play this piece," she said, indicating a piano prelude by Rachmaninoff. Within a month, through diligent practice, he had memorized the piece and could perform it as well as his mother could. True to her word, she allowed him to stop piano lessons. Accordingly, our local congregation and the broader musical world was deprived the talents of a gifted young musician. (I might add that God will not be deprived. Today, this man's twelve-year-old son is performing widely in churches and as the piano soloist for a youth symphony in a large metropolitan area.) A person's inclination can be a guide to being called to certain ministries, but it is only one factor among many. Pastors and church leaders can perform an important function by being on the lookout for people's talents and finding appropriate ways to nurture and utilize these gifts within the life of the congregation and the church. Such nurture may ease the minds of gifted people and move them from reluctance to joyful service.

The sense of call to serve in particular ministries, whether as a layperson or clergy, comes first from God. It has to do with our talents and gifts for ministry. It also has to do with our level of comfort and our inclination to serve. But how does one discern the call? By whose voice does it come? Professor William Willimon of Duke Divinity School tells his beginning ministry students the story of a young seminarian who, during Willimon's days at Yale Divinity School, listened to a lecture on vocation by Professor James Dittes. Based on his research, Dittes had concluded that people entered the ministry largely on the basis of type. Seminarians seemed primarily to be people who had been what he termed "little adults" as children. They typically filled positions of responsibility such as crossing guards and hall monitors. After the lecture, the young man sought out the professor and confessed that he was distressed at what he had heard in the lecture. He felt that the professor had challenged his sense of call to the ordained ministry. The young man acknowledged that he had been one of the "little adults" as a youngster. Nonetheless, he felt that his call to be a pastor came from an external source— especially through the comments he had received from the elderly women in his congregation. When he relayed this concern to his professor, the professor replied, "Do you think that God has stopped calling people into the ministry through little old ladies? Why, that's always been one of God's best approaches."

Whether it comes through the voice of the pastor, the chair of a congregational committee, or the person in the pew, the call to serve in particular ministries does often come through people who are observant enough to note in others the kinds of skills that various ministries call for. We serve by the endowment of God, at the activation of the Spirit, and for the good of the church. We are called to these ministries by the discernment of our gifts, the desire to use them as God intends, and by the voice of the people who call us forth to use them in particular capacities.

There is another important element of discernment: we need to know when to decline a call to serve. We may be interested in a particular ministry and feel gifted for it but decline because our gifts are not sufficiently honed to serve well. Singers know this, that they may have the vocal gifts to perform a particular piece, but their voice is not in good shape due to a cold or lack of use. We may also decline to serve because we feel we have not been adequately trained for a ministry. Or, like Janet, we may feel that we have not been given sufficient time to prepare. At times we may simply be too busy to undertake another task. All of these are legitimate reasons to decline an invitation to serve. When making confession, we often repent of "things left undone." Yet saying no to a request to serve is not necessarily a sin. It may simply be good judgment.

SPIRITUAL GIFTS FOR READING SCRIPTURE IN PUBLIC WORSHIP

What are the qualifications of those who are well gifted for the service of reading Scripture in public? Several years ago, Father Robert Hovda wrote a book for clergy on the role of presiding in worship. In *Strong, Loving, and Wise*, he identified seven qualifications for serving in this ministry. With slight modification to accommodate the differences in roles, I find that these qualifications match those that are useful for ministers who perform the role of lector in worship.

Father Hovda's first suggestion is that ministers have depth and commitment of faith. The public reading of Scripture is not a role to be given to a seeker or the novice. Because the Word of God is the source and foundation of our faith, it needs to be read with conviction. The listener will expect that those who read God's Word in public know the territory, are familiar with not only the biblical material but also the faith that comes through it. Reading the Scriptures is the first order of proclamation. The message of God's promise is proclaimed by people who know the promise and have had their lives changed by it.

The second qualification is native talent. For the presider, Hovda indicates the need for the talents of openness to others, respect for the gifts of others, and willingness to share ministerial responsibilities. For the lector, other talents are helpful. Among them are these eight:

1. A lector should possess a capacity and desire for studying the Bible. An important first step in reading well is understanding the background of the text and interpreting its meaning. At times it is also necessary to craft a brief word of introduction based on your study so that the context of a reading or the flow of its logic can be explained to the assembly.
2. The lector should be prayerfully open to interpretation of the text. Good interpretation is always a function of careful study and inspiration of the Spirit.
3. The reader of Scripture in worship should possess confidence to speak boldly the Word of God. It is humbling to be the vehicle of what Charles Bartow calls "God's human speech." Yet humility implies that the reader can proclaim the Word with the confidence of a herald who knows the importance of the message.
4. The lector should have a clear, pleasant voice.
5. The reader should have vocal facility, the ability to utilize the full range of modulation, volume, and tone. At times the reader may want to whisper "Be still, and know that I am God" (Psalm 46:10). At other times she may want to shout, as did Peter, "I do not know the man!" (Matthew 26:74).
6. Lectors should possess liturgical presence. In theatrical settings, this is known as stage presence. It is the ability to present oneself confidently and unselfconsciously and to use one's body appropriately in the rendering of a part. It involves knowing how to use the eyes effectively and the use of face and body gestures.

7. The lector should possess the capacity for abandonment. This is the ability to lay aside personal concerns and the awareness of self so that one's full attention, voice, and body are available as resources for interpreting the text in its reading. Abandonment also has to do with a reader's ability to employ and judge the effect of performance techniques. Experienced performers learn that what may seem to the performer like exaggerated levels of technique are actually perceived by listeners as being just right. For example, in learning to read slowly, the inexperienced reader may feel that he or she is proceeding at a preposterously slow pace, while the listener may perceive the pace to be too fast.

8. The lector should be transparent in the reading. The *persona* of the text is not that of the reader. Nor is it, in many cases, even that of the author. The Prophets wrote their oracles in the voice of God. The Gospel writers recorded the words of Jesus and other characters. The psalmists wrote in many voices. The reader of these texts should be as hidden in their presentations of them as the authors are in writing them. It is God's Word that should be heard, and not the word, opinion, or persona of the lector.

As noted in the introduction, talents are God-given capacities that enable us to accomplish things. Most people have a little talent for many things. Most people also have a high degree of talent for a few particular things. In a congregation the talents associated with the ministry of serving as lector will be possessed by many people to greater and lesser degrees. While many people might learn to serve well in this ministry, there will be a few who are most naturally gifted for this task. They will take more naturally to the techniques that make for effective public reading. These people might make the best teachers for passing their skills on to others.

The third qualification that Hovda identifies is desire and the feeling of call. As demonstrated above, the inclination to serve in this ministry and the call to do so come as much from the observation and invitation of others as they do from the assessment of one's personal inventory of gifts. Above all, the call and desire to serve derive from God who uses our talents as needed to meet the church's needs.

Fourth, lectors have a need for adequate training. A starting point for such training might be a class or workshop held by gifted readers who can impart their knowledge and skill to willing students. Resources such as this book and those resources listed in appendix B can further help to prepare people for this ministry.

The fifth qualification for the public reading of Scripture is accomplishment or proved aptitude. Skills for this ministry are not meant to be learned by baptism under fire. Working with a teacher or mentor and practicing the skills take time. A period of apprenticeship can enable a reader to learn the craft, provide an arena for evaluation, and make one ready for performing this ministry in public.

Hovda identifies the sixth qualification for service as a mandate from the faith community. This may come from the voice of the pastor or an appointed church leader. They may call upon people to serve because they recognize in them the polished skills of an effective lector. Or, they may call upon people in whom they discern the potential to become effective readers and offer them the opportunity to be trained to serve. Sometimes individuals, discovering in themselves the desire and appropriate skills, will step forward to offer their service. Congregations that take this ministry seriously will be both receptive and careful in accepting eager volunteers. They may wish to audition a person's reading skills and offer them additional training before extending the invitation to serve publicly in this ministry.

The final qualification Hovda speaks of is important for nearly all areas of ministry: a commitment to continuing education. Any human skill can become rusty through lack of use, or it can become routinized. The commitment to hone one's skills will enable the lector to remain an effective leader in an important worship ministry. As an inducement for the upkeep of their skills, lectors should remember that there is nothing less at stake in their public reading of Scripture than the faith of the people whom they serve.

SHOULD I SERVE AS A LECTOR IN PUBLIC WORSHIP?

Who should accept the invitation to serve in this ministry of the Word? The answer: *you*, if you and others identify in you a hunger for God's Word and a desire to proclaim it clearly and boldly to God's people; *you*, if you have a capacity and desire for careful biblical study; *you*, if you have a clear voice and an interest in developing its use for public address; *you*, if you have the time to devote to learning the skills of effective public reading; and *you*, if you can be unselfconscious in serving so that others can be Christ-conscious in hearing. If you, like Janet, are being called upon for an impromptu performance with time for neither training nor preparation, you might well decline the invitation to serve in this way. Or you might decline for other suitable reasons. The goal in this chapter has been to give people a means by which to evaluate their call to serve as lector in worship. Whether a person accepts the invitation to serve in this way or declines, the church is served when people weigh their gifts carefully and make decisions about their Christian service based on a sense of call. How beautiful are we, the body of Christ, when we function in harmony according to how we have been fashioned.

QUESTIONS FOR GROUP DISCUSSION

1. What are the talents with which you have been endowed? How have you used them in your public life?

2. What do you perceive as your spiritual gifts? Which of them will equip you for the ministry of reading Scripture in worship?

3. What skills do you possess that will aid you in this ministry? For which skills do you most require training?

4. What are the attributes of those you observe doing this ministry well?

5. What is the effect on the congregation when this ministry is performed well (or poorly)?

EXERCISES FOR GROUP AND PRIVATE STUDY

1. Have the study group take turns speaking into the church's public address system, preferably from the microphone used by lectors. Recite the Lord's Prayer or the words of a hymn. Have the class listen for each person's vocal timbre (sound quality). Describe the tones being heard so that the speaker gains a sense of the power and potential of his or her own voice. Give the speaker feedback as to the pacing of his or her delivery. Have each speaker experiment with speaking more quickly and more slowly. Let the group evaluate which pace seems most appropriate for each voice and for the type of material being presented. Record the speaking, if possible, so that the speakers can hear themselves as others hear them. Remember that people do not hear internally the same vocal sounds as are projected to others. The typical response is that people who hear themselves

on a recording think their voices sound odd. Encourage one another that their voices do not sound strange to listeners. Try to identify vocal strengths and weaknesses at this early stage.

2. Have each person in the group prepare to tell the story of an incident in his or her life. Each should stand before the group, without notes or the use of a lectern, and tell his or her story in a natural way. Note the natural animation that comes into the face, eyes, and body of the speaker as the story is told. Note, also, the aspects of the storyteller's delivery that indicate the emotional quality of the story. Listen for changes in vocal tone, volume, and intensity. Describe the range of emotions that the speaker's presentation demonstrates or evokes. Note the gestures, facial expressions, and the use of the eyes. As the storyteller becomes involved in the story, where is she or he looking (for example, at the listener, or at imagined people or objects in the story)? Discuss how the aspects of delivery make the speaker's story compelling and easy to listen to. How can these natural and vital elements of storytelling be brought into one's public reading of biblical stories?

3. For private practice, read aloud and record (if possible) the following stories from the Bible. Try to incorporate the natural vitality and enthusiasm that was part of the telling of your own story before the group. As you listen to the playback of your readings, note the vocal and emotional qualities that you employ. Does the way you are using your voice bring out the joy of the first reading or the sorrow of the second? After listening to and analyzing your first recorded readings, repeat the exercise. This time try to exaggerate your use of vocal range, tone, and volume. As you listen to these readings, note that what may have felt to you like exaggeration as

you performed the readings might now be perceived as suitable and appropriate as you become the listener. Repeat the exercise as necessary. If you wish, bring the tape to the study group and play your best readings for group evaluation.

First Reading:

Then all Israel gathered together to David at Hebron and said, "See, we are your bone and flesh. For some time now, even while Saul was king, it was you who commanded the army of Israel. The LORD your God said to you: It is you who shall be shepherd of my people Israel, you who shall be ruler over my people Israel." So all the elders of Israel came to the king at Hebron, and David made a covenant with them at Hebron before the LORD. And they anointed David king over Israel, according to the word of the LORD by Samuel. (1 Chronicles 11:1-3)

Second Reading:

At that very hour some Pharisees came and said to him, "Get away from here, for Herod wants to kill you." [Jesus] said to them, "Go and tell that fox for me, 'Listen, I am casting out demons and performing cures today and tomorrow, and on the third day I finish my work. Yet today, tomorrow, and the next day I must be on my way, because it is impossible for a prophet to be killed outside of Jerusalem.' Jerusalem, Jerusalem, the city that kills the prophets and stones those who are sent to it! How often have I desired to gather your children together as a hen gathers her brood under her wings, and you were not willing!" (Luke 13:31-34)

Chapter 2

THIS IS THE WORD
OF THE LORD

Let us therefore hear the Gospel, just as if we were listening to the Lord Himself present: nor let us say, O happy they who were able to see Him! because there were many of them who saw, and also killed Him; and there are many among us who have not seen Him, and yet have believed. For the precious truth that sounded forth from the mouth of the Lord was both written for our sakes, and preserved for our sakes, and recited for our sakes, and will be recited also for the sake of our prosperity, even until the end of the world.
— St. Augustine, *Homilies on the Gospel of John*, 30.1

*I*t is hard to know whom to believe these days. If we believe the advertisements that bombard us, we cannot be complete or happy individuals unless we dye our hair, drive the right car, shop at the right stores, lose weight, drink the right soda, or own the latest computer. If we believe the words of those running for public office, each candidate is a sterling example of integrity and compassion while his or her opponents are unreliable, selfishly motivated, and of questionable character. The truth appears to be one of several rhetorical options in human communication today, and there is little moral guidance offered by the public figures who are most admired. More than at any time in history we are assailed with words. Which words are true? Which are insignificant? Which are life-changing? Which are life-giving? Which are life-threatening? I recently heard a television ad advising me to watch a particular news magazine show that featured an interview with a retiring sitcom star. The interview, I was promised, would change my life. I rather doubted it. But certain words do have the power to change our lives. If only we could find a way to elevate them and give them a decent hearing.

As Christians, we believe that God's Word will change us.

We trust in the power of the Holy Spirit to work in the Word, bringing faith and transformation. We hope that the Word of God is not some dead letter but a living word that continues to bring new life to the church, and regeneration to individuals who hear it. For people overwhelmed by careless, clever, entertaining, and deceitful words, we know there is one word worth believing. It is God's Word of truth and love. Many of us read and study it privately and are fed by it. But we also need to lift it up in the midst of God's people and to pronounce it aloud as a living word. This is what we attempt to do when God's people gather in worship.

GOD AMONG US IN THE WORD

In many worship settings, as the Scripture reading is concluded, the lector makes a bold statement in these or similar words: "This is the word of the Lord." These words are bold because they are true. The reader has spoken trustworthy words that come from the voice of God. As Augustine said, when we listen to the reading of Scripture, it is as if the Lord is present among us. That is why we often stand for the reading of the Gospel lesson. We do this not because Christ is being *spoken of* in the reading, but because Christ is *present* in it. Discernment of this presence is a matter of faith; it cannot be known by sight or touch. Our trust in his presence relies on Jesus' promise in Matthew 18:20: "For where two or three are gathered in my name, I am there among them." We rely also on the words of John, who revealed that God's "Word became flesh and lived among us" (John 1:14). When God's Word comes alive in public reading, it is, to borrow an image from Dietrich Bonhoeffer, as if Christ steps down from the text to walk among the people. God's Word: of all the words that we hear, these are the words to believe; these are the words that will change our lives.

When a lector proclaims God's Word in worship, it should be remembered that the words spoken are not merely sounds added to the sea of verbiage that surrounds us. Nor are they the reader's or some historic writer's words. Scripture read aloud is nothing less than the Word of God presented as if in God's voice. (Recall the phrase from the previous chapter, that this is "God's human speech.") The church has always understood it to be so. Swiss theologian Karl Barth put it directly: "The fact of the canon tells us simply that the church has regarded these scriptures as the place where we can expect to hear the voice of God." If anything would give a person reason to decline to serve as a reader of Scripture in public worship, it may be this. To serve as God's own voice and to be the bearer of a word of timeless truth, such a charge may seem too great a responsibility. Even the prophet Moses knew this fear and felt inadequate to speak for God. In Exodus, as God recruits Moses at the burning bush, Moses responds: "O my Lord, I have never been eloquent, neither in the past nor even now that you have spoken to your servant; but I am slow of speech and slow of tongue" (4:10). But God would not allow for the word to go unspoken. God said to Moses, "Who gives speech to mortals? Who makes them mute or deaf, seeing or blind? Is it not I, the LORD? Now go, and I will be with your mouth and teach you what you are to speak" (4:11-12). Like Moses, we might well be reluctant to speak God's Word in public. But God's Word will not be silenced, and God still calls people forth to proclaim it. If we are so called, we can trust that God will give us what Moses was given—the words to speak and the capacity to speak them. With trust in God's promises for presence and a godly message, those of us who are called to read

Scripture in worship undertake a great responsibility that ought to be borne with care.

Our purpose here is not to frighten or intimidate prospective lectors. Rather, it is to underscore the significance of the task and to encourage lectors to approach it with reverence and diligence. One of the most frequent criticisms of worship that I hear, even at services of worship in seminary chapels, is that the reading of Scripture is done so poorly. Poor reading often results not from any lack of skill by the readers. Certainly people being called into the ordained ministry and trained in the arts of preaching ought to possess the basic skills for Scripture reading. The problem is lack of attention to this mode of proclamation. The readings are often rendered so as to suggest that they are an insignificant or a secondary part of the service of worship. When scriptures are read aloud without preparation, phrases can be bungled and tricky words mispronounced; thoughtless phrasing and interpretation of the text can make its meaning unintelligible. A student recently reported an even more thoughtless mistake. She heard a lector read in such a way as to ridicule the text. Because this reader could not pronounce certain biblical names and did not care to learn, he said, "So being sent out by the Holy Spirit, they went down to *blah, blah, blah*; and from there they sailed to Cyprus. When they arrived at *blah, blah, blah,* they proclaimed the word of God in the synagogues of the Jews." A reader who so mistreats the Word clearly has no sense that God is present as the Word is proclaimed. But the lack of discernment of God's presence is not the only problem. The greater problem is that such irresponsibility is a disservice to God's people. Certainly God's Word has suffered greater insults. But in public worship, ill-prepared readings have an effect on people's spiritual welfare. We need words we can count on. We need readers we can trust to speak God's Word so that its truth shines forth. We do not attempt to read the Scriptures well in worship merely to honor the Word. We attend to these things carefully because people's faith is at stake.

FAITH COMES THROUGH HEARING

The Christian faith is evangelical. This means that it is spread by the transmission of the good news of Jesus Christ. The word can be spread through casual conversation, through personal testimonies among friends, and in any kind of setting. In worship, the word is transmitted more formally—through the word preached and read from the Scriptures. In the book of Acts, we first see the gospel proclaimed in these ways by the apostles. At times the apostles preach to street crowds and privately share the faith with individuals in homes and prisons. At other times, they proclaim the message of Christ in the synagogues and demonstrate how the God of Hebrew Scripture is the God of the gospel. In both situations, people are brought to the faith as the Holy Spirit works through the proclaimed Word. The church began with a few dozen believers and spread to all the known world as the gospel was preached. The pattern continues today. The Holy Spirit brings people to faith chiefly through the sharing of the gospel story. And those who have been given new life in Christ are further transformed by God's Word as it is read, studied, and proclaimed. Through the Word comes an understanding of faithful living, the need for repentance, the desire for forgiveness, and the power to live in selfless love. Faith is born of and nurtured by the Word. A strong tenet of the Christian faith is that new life comes through hearing God's Word proclaimed.

People gather in worship to hear this Word and to be open to the ways that it can transform their lives. If it is poorly presented, if it is mumbled, hurried, or inexpressibly rendered, it can fail to be heard or understood. One might argue that the Holy Spirit can use it to bring about faith and forgiveness even if the Word is poorly presented. Perhaps this is true, yet it is no license for carelessness. How much more will the Spirit be able to use a word well spoken?

Others may argue that a story simply told will not have the power over people that such stories once had. People have become so accustomed to information that is reduced to sound bites, clever slogans, and thirty-second television spots that they may not have the attention span to absorb penetrating stories. The lector, no matter how polished, is seldom a match for the elegant, chic, or trendy spokesperson that delivers most of the information we receive from television. How can the public reading of stories change people's lives? It happens today as it always has. If a story is well told, it has the power to captivate listeners, bringing new insight and drawing them into a world that is not their own. One can see this at work regularly with children. Of all people, they are most susceptible to boredom and the need for stimulation. Many children today have never known a life without electronic multisensory media. The Internet, with all its phenomenal resources, is as common to them as the telephone. If they want stimulation, there are video games, movies, chat rooms, and Web sites literally at their fingertips. Occasionally, they even wander outside to play with one another. Their world is characterized by endless opportunity for overstimulation. Still, there is something in children that longs for human touch and the sound of a personal voice. Observe what happens when children are given the opportunity to hear a well-told story. Like people of all ages, they lean forward to catch each word, and their imaginations take them on journeys to unknown worlds. All of the sensory imagery that they need is supplied as the tale unfolds and the words paint pictures in their minds. We often laugh over the stories our parents tell us when they boast about hardships they suffered as they were growing up. Yet how refreshing it is for a parent to hear a young child say, "Mama, tell me again that story about what happened when you were a little girl." For a few moments there is a brief escape from the world of computers, television, and impersonal communication. Deep calls to deep when people face one another and unfold a good story between them.

If a story still has the power to captivate us, then how much more will the biblical story have the capacity to change us if it draws us into itself and becomes the vehicle for the Holy Spirit to work on our hearts? Our goal as lectors is not just to read the story but to read it well, filling it with energy, life, and sensual imagery. We attempt to read the story so as to create a world too enticing to ignore. In many worship settings, people are invited to follow along with the reader from pew Bibles or lessons printed in bulletins. While this is a fine way to draw people into partic-ipation in the scriptural texts, imagine a reading presented so vividly that it would make following along in the text as unnec-essary as following a movie script in a theater. If faith comes through hearing, how crucial it is for the lector to be aware of God's presence in his or her work and to attempt to present to God's people a living word to hear.

GETTING OUT OF THE WAY

To proclaim a living word means that the reader needs to pre-pare carefully; yet the purpose is not to demonstrate one's prepa-ration. Most of us have witnessed the mistake of a reader who so overdoes the performance of a text that the principal thing we see is the actor. We gather in worship to hear the Word of God and to have an encounter with Christ. We do not come to be entertained by a creative presentation or stunned by a bit of technique. The reader's goal is to perform the Word in such a way that God's voice comes through.

Often the word *performance*, as relating to worship, is under-stood in negative terms. It may suggest entertainment or theatrics. But as a means for describing the lector's role, it is a useful word. *To perform well* means to allow the words to come through with clarity. We do our best when performing is in ser-vice to the Word. The reader who draws attention to himself or herself, either through lack of preparation or dramatics, stands in the way of the Word's connection with the listener. The goal is to use technique to get out of the way. The thoughtful lector will study the text, think about how it should be delivered, rehearse the reading, and prepare body and voice for an effective presentation or performance of the text. Beneath these basic elements of preparation are two underlying principles of performance: interpretation and abandonment.

ORAL INTERPRETATION OF SCRIPTURE

We may assume that interpretation of a biblical text is the preacher's job. True enough. But oral interpretation of Scripture is the reader's job. We cannot avoid it. Just as in reading poetry or fiction aloud, there are elements of oral presentation that provide meaning and clarity. It is impossible to read material aloud so as to make it devoid of interpretation. Sometimes readers will argue that God's Word is so important, they do not want to add anything of their own interpretation to the text. They read, then, in a detached, objective manner, expecting God to use the Word as God will. The problem here is that a detached reading of the text actually does give a subjective interpretation. The reader's detachment suggests that the lesson is dull or unimportant. Even if a lector prepares carefully and does his or her best to pronounce the text precisely and clearly but does not become involved in the text as a living word, the reader will give a false impression of its meaning. The Word of God is vital and needs to be fully embraced and passionately proclaimed. Any detached reading is a *mis*reading of Scripture; any attempt at avoiding interpretation of God's Word is a *mis*interpretation of it. There is no such thing as a neutral reading of a text. As an example, consider the following text from Luke 4:

> All spoke well of him and were amazed at the gracious words that came from his mouth. They said, "Is not this Joseph's son?" He said to them, "Doubtless you will quote to me this proverb, 'Doctor, cure yourself!' And you will say, 'Do here also in your hometown the things that we have heard you did at Capernaum.' " And he said, "Truly I tell you, no prophet is accepted in the

prophet's hometown. But the truth is, there were many widows in Israel in the time of Elijah, when the heaven was shut up three years and six months, and there was a severe famine over all the land; yet Elijah was sent to none of them except to a widow at Zarephath in Sidon. There were also many lepers in Israel in the time of the prophet Elisha, and none of them was cleansed except Naaman the Syrian." When they heard this, all in the synagogue were filled with rage. They got up, drove him out of the town, and led him to the brow of the hill on which their town was built, so that they might hurl him off the cliff. But he passed through the midst of them and went on his way. (4:22-30)

Just prior to this passage, in his hometown synagogue Jesus has inaugurated his ministry by reading from the words of the prophet Isaiah. He tells the people that Isaiah's words are being fulfilled in their hearing. His congregation is impressed. Local boy makes good. But by the end of this passage, the people of Jesus' hometown turn on him and are so enraged as to want to destroy him. If a modern reader attempted to present this passage in a detached manner, providing no clues as to its interpretation, its sense would be lost. How could Jesus' rhetorical statements and his brief recounting of historical events create such offense? Clearly they could not if they were spoken with indifference. The interpretive result would be that the story would seem to contain a discontinuity in logic. But if the lector reads the passage with a tone of exhortation, and if she emphasizes the exclusionary nature of Jesus' words, then the story makes sense. The people are proud of Jesus so long as the benefit of his ministry is to be spread among his people. However, if there were nothing in it for them, if his miracles and wonders were for foreigners and nonbelievers, then their pride would turn to anger. If Jesus was turning on his own people and challenging their way of life, this was a capital offense. It nearly got him killed. Eventually it did. The reader needs to render this text in a way that unfolds its internal logic.

Not all passages require such pointed emphasis. This example, however, points out a general truth. To read aloud from the Scriptures is to be involved in oral interpretation. It cannot be avoided by reading in a neutral manner in the hope that the Word of God will speak for itself. God calls readers to the public ministry of speaking the Word. As in all proclamation, it is a ministry of interpretation.

How, then, does the lay reader obtain the necessary background to prepare a fair interpretation of a biblical text. Good proclamation, whether it is reading Scripture in worship or preaching from it, begins with two fundamental steps. First, the reader approaches the text in prayer. Trusting that God calls people into this special ministry and provides the gifts to perform effectively, we trust further that God will provide insight into the text so that it can be rendered with clarity and meaning. Second, the lay reader studies the text and its surrounding material to understand its setting and more fully grasp its significance. The process of biblical study and the tools for discovery will be more carefully examined in the next chapter.

ABANDONMENT

How do well-prepared readers perform texts so as to get out of the texts' way? They do so with a sense of abandon. Public speaking, it is often said, is among the most stressful of human situations. What makes it difficult is the sense that all eyes and ears in an audience are upon the speaker. Accompanying the audience's attention is the prospect of judgment. The speaker is subject to the audience's assessment of his or her looks, dress, knowledge of material, vocal quality, and stage presence. Being self-conscious of these things is a natural reaction to performing in front of an audience. It is difficult to mask, becomes another element of a speaker's behavior for the audience to notice, and thus places the speaker in the way of the message. The goal in reading Scripture in worship is for the listener to become Christ-conscious. The reader abandons himself or herself in service to the Word.

There is an interesting paradox that takes place in performing. On the one hand, the more a person is concerned about how he acts or appears, the more he tends to restrict his involvement in the performance. On the other hand, the more a person gives herself over to the demands of a role, the more natural she appears and the better she performs. The intimidated performer gets in the way of the performance. The abandoned performer lets herself go and uses all the capacities of body and voice in service of the task. She blends her whole being into the performance and becomes transparent in the role. When this happens in reading Scripture in worship, the text and its meaning unfold while the lector recedes as a servant of the Word.

As a pastor, I was surprised by an example of this sense of abandonment one Sunday when our congregation was having a special focus on children in worship. Marilyn, who during the week worked as a kindergarten teacher, was not able to participate as a reader in worship on Sunday mornings because she usually played the church organ. But on this occasion her interest in the special children's service resulted in Marilyn's participation in leading the service. For the children's sermon, Marilyn read a story from a children's Bible. As I listened to her reading, I was struck by how naturally modulated and animated her voice was. She read with energy, enthusiasm, precise diction, and a pleasing range of vocal tone and modulation. At first I was surprised that Marilyn had such fine interpretive skills. On second thought, it occurred to me that this was precisely what she did every day of the week as a teacher. She read to children who sat captivated by her rendering of stories. She had learned to do this with confidence and lack of self-consciousness. She had learned to use the techniques of oral interpretation in the perfect classroom, where clarity and meaning were critical and judgment by her audience was nil. Her skill carried over into worship, where Marilyn was able to perform effectively with a remarkable lack of inhibition.

How does the lector acquire such abandonment? It begins, as does the process of interpretation, with prayer. Again, trusting that God calls people into this special ministry, we trust also that God gives us the spiritual gifts to accomplish it well. Prayer and acknowledging that we trust God in this endeavor is the natural starting point, but it is not the only step. The reader would rightly be self-conscious who was not well prepared to use his or her body and voice in service to the Word. Therefore attention is given to issues such as vocal inflection, tonal modulation, pacing of words, and the use of gestures. As a reader practices these things, he or she will become comfortable in their use, knowledgeable as to their effectiveness, and proficient at using these techniques in bringing God's Word forth. Certainly, these techniques can be overdone and can become melodramatic. But sufficient practice and the kind critique of a coach or small-group classmates can help people discern the appropriate ways to make a text come alive. The material in chapters 4 and 5 will address these aspects of interpretive technique.

With the acquisition of such skills and with the confidence that comes through training and practice, lectors will be prepared to step forward to participate in this important ministry of sharing God's Word. Trusting in their call to this ministry and in their capacity for interpretation and effective performance, they can boldly proclaim, "This is the word of the Lord."

QUESTIONS FOR GROUP DISCUSSION

1. Is there a difference between employing techniques for oral interpretation and using "theatrics" in the performance of a reading?
2. Are there modes of public performance for which you feel relaxed? Are there others for which you feel self-conscious? What are the elements that give you confidence or fear as you perform in public roles?
3. How does the word *performance* strike you as it relates to Christian worship? What aspects of performance seem inappropriate for worship? What types of performances in public life can serve as useful analogues for the ways we properly perform in worship?
4. Do dress and appearance have an impact on the effective oral interpretation of scriptural texts?

EXERCISES FOR GROUP AND PRIVATE STUDY

1. Taking a cue from the story of Marilyn (as related above), begin to practice oral interpretation of a story by reading a children's book to the class. Let the reader pretend that he or she is actually reading to children. Note how naturally expressive our voices tend to be when we read to little ones. Try to bring this level of energy and creativity into the reading of this story before the group. To what extent can this type of exaggerated expression be used in reading Scriptures in worship?
2. As an exercise in abandonment, try reading aloud the sentence below in the ways indicated. The results may seem awkward, strange, even silly to the class, but the object is for each person to gain practice in using his or her entire

vocal capacity in service of the text. Try accompanying each reading with exaggerated hand gestures that match the tone of the reading.

"The reign of Richard the Great was fraught with terrible tragedy."

—spoken entirely in falsetto

—spoken by rolling or trilling all the "r" sounds

—spoken in a deep voice

—spoken in a flat tone, devoid of emotion

—spoken in a sing-song manner

—spoken as a smooth, unbroken phrase

—spoken in a feigned foreign accent

—spoken in a whiny, nasal tone

—spoken to suggest a question

—spoken to suggest disgust

—spoken in a staccato manner

—sung or chanted on a single pitch

3. Read aloud the following lines from the psalms. Try to match your vocal tone to the mood of each piece.

> O sing to the LORD a new song,
>   for he has done marvelous things.
> His right hand and his holy arm
>   have gotten him victory. (Psalm 98:1)

> By the rivers of Babylon—
>   there we sat down and there we wept
>   when we remembered Zion.
> On the willows there
>   we hung up our harps. (Psalm 137:1-2)

O LORD, you God of vengeance,
   you God of vengeance, shine forth!
Rise up, O judge of the earth;
   give to the proud what they deserve! (Psalm 94:1-2)

4. For private practice: As opportunity allows, read to children. Practice using a range of vocal expressiveness. Try using different voices for characters in the story. Pay special attention to the ways that vocal inflection can underscore or clarify meaning of the text.

Chapter 3

APPROACHING THE TEXT

Who can know the infinity of seeds, when in a single one are contained forests of forests and thence seeds in infinite number? Likewise, out of Scriptures may be drawn an infinite number of interpretations which none but God can comprehend. For as new seeds come forth from plants, so also from Scriptures come forth new interpretations and meanings, and thereby are sacred Scriptures distinct from everything else. Hence, in relation to the interpretations yet to be drawn, we may compare to a single drop from the sea all those that have been drawn so far.

> —Saint Bonaventure, *Collations of the Six Days,*
> *Thirteenth Collation*

If Bonaventure is correct, how could any interpreter of the Bible ever know that he or she has it right? As suggested in the last chapter, these things are revealed in part to the reader and interpreter who begins with prayer and does the homework. Preachers hope they have it right when they stand to speak the Word of God to a waiting, hungry people. Indeed, they pray diligently that they get it right, for nothing less is at stake than the faith of God's people. But prayer alone does not release the full meaning of a text. The infinite seeds of interpretation are unlocked when the reader or preacher becomes a student who looks carefully at a text. The hope is that through prayer the Holy Spirit will guide the hand of the interpreter, and the seeds of interpretation will be revealed through careful study. The purpose of this chapter is to focus on the tools that students of the Bible can use as they approach a text that is to be read aloud in public worship.

WHAT DO YOU NEED TO KNOW?

In order to bring out a proper interpretation of a biblical text, the reader will want to look at a number of things, such as who wrote the text, when it was written, how it might have been transmitted, how it relates to other texts in the Bible, and so on. This is similar to the kind of work that preachers learn to do when they take Bible and preaching courses in seminary. They learn to enter into a rigorous investigation to be certain that the kernel of interpretation they bring forth in the sermon is godly and honest. At this point I need to mention one technical term—one that is commonly used among preachers and Bible scholars—in order to demonstrate the connection between preaching and oral interpretation of Scripture: *exegesis* (pronounced *ex-eh-jee-sis*). It means, simply, the research that a biblical interpreter does in order to understand a text as fully as possible. The process is not intended to do what an anonymous skeptic has suggested, to *ex-out-Jesus*. Rather, it is undertaken to reveal those things about a text that will best help the reader understand it. Because it suggests a process that is technical and exhaustive, the term *exegesis* sometimes distresses Bible students and budding preachers, who might prefer to use a friendlier term: *discovery*. Whichever term is used, the goal is the same—to do enough study about a text so as to understand it well and bring forth a fitting interpretation. New Testament scholar Richard Hays has found a straightforward way to define the process. Exegesis, he says, is any "close reading of a text."

We need not be put off by the thought of a "close reading" of a Bible text, because it is the kind of reading that the average person does regularly, even daily. It is, for example, the kind of work we do whenever we read a newspaper. We look carefully at the front page and know that what we find on it has a basis in fact and recent history. On the editorial page, we realize that we are reading a different kind of material and know we are free to disagree with a writer's opinion as stated there. On the personals page, we understand that the words "consuming fire" might not have the same meaning as they would if they were found in a story on the front page. We know that if an international story mentions a country we are unfamiliar with, we need to look it up on a current map in order to understand the report. We typically compare newspaper reports to those we get from television and other sources. And we naturally adjust our interpretation of a story to allow for a particular writer's slant, bias, or audience. In other words, we commonly do a close reading of newspaper texts and interpret the material in light of what we know or what we can discover about them. When dealing with the Bible, we are to employ similar techniques in order to get at a text's meaning.

Preachers have the responsibility to dig into a text rather thoroughly because they need to craft a message that springs from the soil of a text and remains true to its theology, form, and function. Lectors have a more direct task to accomplish: they are to present texts plainly and with interpretive sensitivity. The only layer of interpretation a reader adds is that which comes through the performance of the actual words. Therefore, though lectors may follow the same path of discovery as preachers, they will not need to research a text with such painstaking effort. A simplified process of discovery will usually yield sufficient information to render a faithful oral interpretation of a biblical text.

What would happen if this discovery process were neglected? Can this have a negative effect on the oral interpretation? Indeed, it can and all too frequently does. Examples of textual misinterpretation abound. How often do we see a reader in worship launch into a complex or detailed passage of Scripture without providing a statement to give the listeners a frame of reference? Commonly the result is that the text has little meaning because the listener cannot tell what issue is being addressed by the author or how it relates to the material that surrounds it. Or, how often do worshipers hear readers stumble through a text, tripping on the pronunciation of biblical names? And imagine the challenge the listener faces in understanding a text when it is read by someone who fails to calculate its grammatical structure or its syntactical sense? The responsible lector will want to spend time with a text, figuring out what he or she needs to know about it in order to render a clear and comprehensible presentation of it.

What does the thoughtful reader look for in preparing a public reading of a biblical text? A reader's interpretation will be guided by some knowledge of the following categories of discovery:

Author and Setting. Knowing something about where a text comes from, who might have written it, and how it might have been used in its original setting can provide many insights for oral interpretation. For example, should the psalms all be read with the confidence of a king, or might one be read differently if it is likely that David is not its author? Or, what difference would it make in a reading of Ephesians if it is uncertain that Paul wrote it himself? Biblical scholarship has been discovering new information about the Scriptures for decades, and some of the old traditions about certain texts' authorship are being helpfully revised. This material is largely available to readers who wish to look closely at a text.

Form. Just as in reading a newspaper, it is useful to know something about a biblical text's form. It would be folly to interpret a car advertisement's bold claims as if they were in the form of front-page news. Likewise, it is inappropriate to read a Gospel parable as if it were a historical event. Clearly Jesus chose to unfold the truth about the kingdom of God through the use of fictional tales. Similarly, it is unwise to read the first chapter of Genesis as scientific or historical record if it was written in the form of a poem that was intended to describe God's relationship to creation.

Source. Having some knowledge of a text's connection to other parts of the Bible is useful in determining how it should be interpreted orally. Sometimes one section of Scripture will be derived from material contained in another portion of the Bible. What difference would it make in one's reading of the Passion story in Matthew if the reader discovered that Jesus' words from the cross, "My God, my God, why have you forsaken me?" are a quotation from Psalm 22? A careful reader will observe that New Testament writers often borrow phrases or bits of poetry from the Old Testament. How might it affect one's reading of a text if the person has discovered that the text moves from the author's prose into a poetic section borrowed from some other place in Scripture? It also appears that the Gospel writers Matthew and Luke borrowed heavily from Mark as one of their chief sources for material. In order to draw out a particular author's intention, the careful reader will seek to understand how one Gospel rendition differs from the others.

Audience. Here it is helpful for a reader to understand who the biblical author is writing to or the reasons for the material's creation. In many cases there are particular community needs that biblical authors address in their work. When Mark writes the story of Jesus, it is told with great urgency seemingly because Mark is addressing a church under persecution. How might that urgency be relayed in one's reading? When Matthew retells some of Mark's stories, he often borrows phrases and images from the Old Testament because his audience is Jewish, and he seems to be establishing a connection between their traditional faith and faith in Jesus as the promised Messiah. When Paul writes angrily to the Corinthian church in 1 Corinthians, it is useful to know something of the town of Corinth, its local religions and perversions, and the kinds of difficulty this congregation seems to have encountered.

Textual Environment. A key element to understanding the message of a particular text is to determine how it fits into the overall picture of a given author's work. Should a parable, for example, be interpreted differently when it occurs near the beginning of a Gospel writer's work as opposed to when it occurs later in the story of Jesus' ministry? That is, does the imminence of the Passion add layers of meaning to interpretation of certain texts? And, for the interpretation of the first chapter of Acts, how useful would it be to know that the author also wrote the Gospel of Luke? A good way to determine the textual environment of a passage is to read a significant portion of Scripture that precedes and follows an isolated text. This will give the careful reader a sense of the text's flow and place in the overall work. One might even outline the material (both the text and that which surrounds it) in order to gain perspective.

Alternative Readings and Translations. Those who are able to look at a text in its original language (Hebrew for Old Testament material, and Greek for New Testament) can take note of the so-called "variant" readings that have been found among the collections of early versions of biblical texts. Some ancient versions of a particular book read significantly differently than others; some have portions that seem to be added or deleted, others are incomplete or damaged. Laypeople who read Scripture in public worship will usually need to rely on the work of Bible translators to arrive at appropriate conclusions about textual variations. But there is a related question that is useful for the lector to consider: what are the different ways that modern translators have dealt with a given text and its variants? Some translators will choose to include variations others leave out. And, naturally, each translating team will arrive at a unique way to render a text in English. For example, there is usually a great deal of similarity in two standard English translations, the New Revised Standard Version and the New English Bible translation. Still, some interesting and useful things can be discovered as the translations are compared. Often effective oral interpretation grows out of the knowledge gained from looking at how several different translations treat an appointed passage. A clue to the translators' intentions can sometimes be found in reading the introduction or preface. A Bible edition's introduction usually indicates the particular focus the translators have in mind as they approach their work. This shapes the choices they make about how to deal with variations and how to render the Scriptures in the most appropriate English. Note especially that some Bible translations are intended to be *paraphrases* of the original texts. The wording of paraphrases is usually simple and clear because the translators add a level of theological interpretation before rendering the texts in English. In other words, the interpreters solve textual mysteries and make decisions about the biblical material before putting it in common, easily understood language. This presents interpretive choices that may not be appropriate in all settings. For this reason, Bible paraphrases may not be the best choice for public reading of Scripture. Still, they serve a useful purpose for the careful reader who wishes to explore as thoroughly as possible the range of interpretation that is possible for an appointed lesson.

WHERE TO LOOK

Where does the lector look to find the kind of information that is useful in determining how to prepare for reading a text in worship? Several kinds of resources can be used in the discovery process. They include the following:

Reference or Study Editions of the Bible. Most Bible translations come in editions that provide a great deal of useful material. A good reference Bible will give cross-references in the page margins, indicating places in Scripture that a given passage relates to. Such Bibles will also provide material in the footnotes that indicates textual problems and variations. These are often identified by words similar to these: "other ancient sources read. . . ." Additionally, reference Bibles contain end material that is filled with useful study tools. They can include lists of Old and New Testament parables and miracles; lists comparing the parables and miracles of Jesus in the four Gospels; outlines and timelines of biblical events; a concordance (in which individual words can be looked up to see where they occur in the Scriptures); a dictionary of biblical terms; a pronunciation guide; and maps of biblical lands from various historical periods. Often reference Bibles also contain material that discusses authorship, historical setting, and theme at the beginning of each book.

Parallel Translations. An extremely useful tool is the Parallel Bible. It is a single volume that places three or four biblical translations side by side for ease of comparison. For example, a parallel edition might place the Revised Standard Version, the New Revised Standard Version, the King James Version, and the New King James Version in four parallel columns. There are also computer resources that allow for the same kind of comparison.

Gospel Parallels. A similar tool is the Gospel parallel, a book containing a single translation (the New Revised Standard Version, for example) that places the four Gospel accounts side by side. The value of this resource is that it allows the researcher to see readily the differences in how the Gospel writers use the basic material of Jesus' life and ministry. Seeing the four versions side by side makes it clear where Luke has embellished a story that Mark tells more succinctly, or where Matthew tells a story in such a way as to appeal to his Jewish audience. It is in looking carefully at a Gospel parallel that it becomes evident that Matthew and Luke seem to use much of the material that is contained in Mark. This has led scholars to surmise that Mark was available to Matthew and Luke as a source document. It also becomes clear that there are large blocks of material in the first three books that do not appear in John. Similarly, it is obvious that there is much material original to John that is not contained in the other Gospels.

Bible Dictionaries. These reference books usually provide more than word definitions. A resource called a *lexicon* is the place preachers turn to for checking on the precise meanings of Greek and Hebrew words. Bible dictionaries are usually more like encyclopedias. They contain articles on words, phrases, places, and names that are found in the Old and New Testaments. A Bible dictionary is a good source for reading up on the authorship of a particular book of the Bible and the historical setting that gave rise to the creation or compilation of the material.

Bible Commentaries. These reference books are indispensable to preachers, who learn both to do their own exegetical work and to check their work against the opinion of established professionals. Writers of biblical commentaries are usually Old or New

Testament scholars who read the original texts carefully, provide useful information about how various words and phrases are to be translated and interpreted, and who draw theological conclusions about the meaning of texts. They explore the same range of issues that the careful preacher considers: Where does a text come from? Who wrote it? What gave rise to its authorship? How was the text originally used? What ancient copies of the text provide the best insight into the author's original intention? What particular circumstances or concerns did the author face that might have shaped the way a passage was written? For the careful reader of a text who does not have the capacity to read the Scriptures in the original languages, the use of commentaries is extremely valuable. In order to allow for the Scriptures to enlighten and surprise them, preachers learn to do their own exegetical work *before* consulting commentaries. Laypeople who read Scripture in public will be well served to turn more quickly to commentaries to learn from experts in biblical research. Because there are countless versions of Bible commentaries, it is a good idea for lay readers to consult with their pastors to determine which commentaries seem most theologically suitable for a given congregation or denomination.

How to Proceed

Given the long list of things to keep in mind during the discovery process, and the numerous resources available for consultation, how can a lay reader know the best procedure for doing the background research that will inform his or her oral interpretation of a text? The process of exegesis is, as Richard Hays says, more art than science. Still, to guide preachers, Hays has crafted a useful method that takes them from text to sermon. This method is explained in an article on exegesis in the *Concise Encyclopedia of Preaching* (Westminster/John Knox Press, 1995). His method, in a simplified version, can also be helpful to the layperson who wishes to do a careful reading of a biblical text in preparation for its public reading.

First, Hays says, read the text carefully. This is a general, non-technical reading designed to give one a sense of how the appointed passage fits into the wider context. Included here is the comparison of several translations of the text. Second, outline the text to get a view of its structure and flow. Third, ask questions that are raised by the text, such as these: *What is the main point? What seems odd or puzzling? What problems are left unresolved? How does the passage challenge prevailing ideas and customs?* Only after doing this initial work, suggests Hays, does the reader turn to reference tools and commentaries to learn about the text in a more technical sense. Here background material can be gathered from maps, Bible dictionaries, and parallels; issues such as text and translation problems can also be considered.

This type of research can take a long time, but it is time well spent. Much is at stake in the public reading of Scripture in worship. The responsible lector will want to discover as much useful information as possible before determining how to perform the text. Crafting a faithful performance of a text will be the focus of the next two chapters. But before leaving this topic, let us consider how some of the material discovered about a text can be presented as a brief introduction to provide the audience with a sense of the text's literary setting.

PREPARING AN INTRODUCTION TO A READING

Not all scripture texts will need to be introduced. Psalms often stand on their own and there is little benefit in preceding their recital with a technical explanation. They are poems, and poetry does not need to be explained. Likewise, many Gospel lessons can be read without introduction. One might simply substitute the word "Jesus" for "he" when a text begins in the midst of a longer story. For example, "They came to *him*" becomes "They came to [Jesus]." It is so much smoother than the oft-used alternative: "They came to *him* (Jesus)."

Some passages, however, do require a little setup in order to make them understandable. In the epistles the writers are often arguing theological issues. If a reading breaks into the middle of such an argument, it is useful to inform listeners about the setting of the discussion. Or, it might be helpful to tell the listeners about an author's audience or how a passage fits into a larger theme or discussion.

When a lector chooses to prepare an introduction for a reading, the following guidelines may be of use:

(1) Keep it short! The worshiper has come to enter into an encounter with the God who is present in the spoken word. This is not the place to demonstrate the readers' erudition or show that their homework has been done. I have seen numerous instances where the introduction has become a mini-sermon, complete with theological interpretation. If a sermon is called for, the preacher will provide it. One or two sentences spoken by the lector is usually enough to set the stage for a reading.

(2) Tell the listeners only that which will make the reading understandable. Good preachers learn to determine what, of all the material they have gathered, needs to be left out. Readers should do the same.

(3) Learn to determine when a reading needs introduction and when it does not. Do not automatically assume that an introduction is necessary. Whenever possible, let the reading stand on its own.

There is much to learn about the Bible. If you wish to serve as a reader in public worship, you might see your first task as becoming a student of the Bible. What you learn will not only prepare you knowledgeably for a fitting oral interpretation of the text but will also be a blessing to your faith as the Scriptures unfold their deeper meaning to you. Remember, we began this chapter with the idea that the seeds of proper interpretation are revealed both through inspiration of the Holy Spirit as an answer to our prayers and through the discipline of study.

QUESTIONS AND SUGGESTIONS FOR GROUP DISCUSSION

1. To what forms of modern literature do the following biblical forms compare (for example, history, fiction, myth, poetry, and so on)? What clues about each story's interpretation might you gather from knowing the kind of form the biblical story represents?

The story of Adam and Eve	The story of Joseph
The story of the ten plagues of the Exodus	The books of Chronicles and Kings
The psalms	The Song of Solomon
The prophecies of Isaiah	The prophecies of Jeremiah
The Gospel narratives	The Gospel parables
The passion narratives	The book of Acts
The epistles	The book of Revelation

2. Where might a lector look for modern examples of good oral interpretation? Are there models at hand that can demonstrate how to render these various forms appropriately? Are there poets, storytellers, teachers, newspeople, or actors in your congregation? Can they be brought in to provide guidance to lectors during their training?

3. What are the tools for discovery available to you? Does your congregation have a library; and, if so, does it include reference material such as commentaries, Bible dictionaries, and study Bibles? If not, can such a collection be started?

4. Invite a pastor to your group meeting and ask her to bring along samples of reference works from her own library. Ask the pastor to discuss how she uses the resources in sermon preparation. Also, ask your pastor which commentaries provide the most fitting interpretation for your congregation or denomination.

5. Discuss with your pastor which translation of the Bible is the most suitable for your setting. Ask him to explain which translations he uses in his own study and which he prefers for use in worship.

EXERCISES FOR GROUP AND PRIVATE STUDY

1. Read the following excerpts from Genesis 1 as if you were recounting scientific or historic fact. Read them a second time as if they were words of poetry written for use in worship. Note the difference in tone that seems appropriate to the different styles of reading. Discuss which seems to be the more appropriate interpretation for this material.

In the beginning when God created the heavens and the earth, the earth was a formless void and darkness covered the face of the deep, while a wind from God swept over the face of the waters. Then God said, "Let there be light"; and there was light. And God saw that the light was good; and God separated the light from the darkness. God called the light Day, and the darkness he called Night. And there was evening and there was morning, the first day.

And God said, "Let there be a dome in the midst of the waters, and let it separate the waters from the waters." So God made the dome and separated the waters that were under the dome from the waters that were above the dome. And it was so. God called the dome Sky. And there was evening and there was morning, the second day.

And God said, "Let the waters under the sky be gathered together into one place, and let the dry land appear." And it was so. God called the dry land Earth, and the waters that were gathered together he called Seas. And God saw that it was good. Then God said, "Let the earth put forth vegetation:

plants yielding seed, and fruit trees of every kind on earth that bear fruit with the seed in it." And it was so. The earth brought forth vegetation: plants yielding seed of every kind, and trees of every kind bearing fruit with the seed in it. And God saw that it was good. And there was evening and there was morning, the third day. (Genesis 1:1-13)

2. Read aloud the following passages from the writings of Paul. To highlight the difference between what he has written and what he is quoting, try to bring a different tone to the portions of the reading that Paul has borrowed from other sources.

First Reading:

What then? Are we any better off? No, not at all; for we have already charged that all, both Jews and Greeks, are under the power of sin, as it is written:
"There is no one who is righteous, not even one;
    there is no one who has understanding,
    there is no one who seeks God.
All have turned aside, together they have become worthless;
    there is no one who shows kindness,
    there is not even one."
"Their throats are opened graves;
    they use their tongues to deceive."
"The venom of vipers is under their lips."
                    (Romans 3:9-13; Psalm 14:1-3 is quoted)

Second Reading:

If then there is any encouragement in Christ, any consolation from love, any sharing in the Spirit, any compassion and sympathy, make my joy complete: be of the same mind, having the same love, being in full accord and of one mind. Do nothing from selfish ambition or conceit, but in humility regard others as better than yourselves. Let each of you look not to your own interests, but to the interests of others. Let the same mind be in you that was in Christ Jesus,

> who, though he was in the form of God,
>   did not regard equality with God
>   as something to be exploited,
> but emptied himself,
>   taking the form of a slave,
>   being born in human likeness.
> And being found in human form,
>   he humbled himself
>   and became obedient to the point of death—
> even death on a cross.
> (Philippians 2:1-8; some scholars see verses 5-8 as lines
> from a Christian song known to Paul and his audience)

3. For homework, prepare a brief introduction for one of the two foregoing lessons. Try to prepare your listeners by giving just enough information to help them in their understanding of the text. In class, let each participant read his or her introduction aloud. Spend time discussing and evaluating each presentation. Remember, here is the place for honest feedback. It should be offered graciously but truthfully, if it is to help participants learn.

Chapter 4

EMBODYING THE WORD

In the beginning was the Word, and the Word was with God, and the Word was God. He was in the beginning with God. All things came into being through him, and without him not one thing came into being. What has come into being in him was life, and the life was the light of all people. The light shines in the darkness, and the darkness did not overcome it. . . . And the Word became flesh and lived among us, and we have seen his glory, the glory as of a father's only son, full of grace and truth.

—John 1:1-5, 14

*T*he Gospel writer John tells us here that the *Word* became flesh to dwell among us. This is the first of John's great metaphors for Christ. (Others include Jesus as the Bread of Life, the Great Shepherd, and the Vine.) But to call Jesus the Word is *more* than metaphor. Christians believe that when he became flesh, Jesus was both God and man. This means that every word that Jesus spoke was God's word. Therefore to say that Jesus is the Word is simply to acknowledge that the Word of God was embodied in a real physical sense.

Today, the presence of Christ dwells in the Word when it is read and proclaimed in worship. But this is a less tangible presence. Nonetheless, the Word *is* embodied physically. It occurs when a member of the body of Christ, to use Paul's great metaphor for the church, steps forward to read the Scriptures.

The reader becomes the embodiment of the Word. The Word becomes flesh again as the lector lends his or her body to the moment of proclamation. For this reason, the faithful reader will want to learn how to use the body in this important task.

Reading Scripture in worship goes beyond the mere use of the voice. Readings come alive most when lectors employ their whole persons in the presentation of God's Word. In particular, embodiment of the Word involves good breathing, vocal production and resonance, the use of the eyes, and certain types of gestures. On rare occasions, it might also involve movement of the entire body, as when a person memorizes and acts out a portion of Scripture. This type of presentation will be addressed briefly in appendix A. The focus of this chapter is on the reader's use of the upper body (lungs, voice, head, eyes, and hands) to make the Word come alive.

BREATH PRODUCTION AND CONTROL

When God breathed into Adam's nostrils the breath of life, Adam became a living soul (Genesis 2:7)—and a speaking person. Without breath, there is no voice and no word. Learning to use the breath effectively is the first element in speaking well and making the Word come alive. Chiefly, it involves two things: good posture and muscle control.

Posture. To stand erect, with shoulders square, enables the lungs to fill to capacity when a breath is drawn. Bending over or stooping the shoulders constricts the chest area and limits the amount of air one can inhale. Try this simple exercise: As you sit reading, bend forward and drop your shoulders. Now take as deep a breath as possible and say "ah." Note that your breath is necessarily shallow and that your voice is not strong. Now, still sitting, straighten your back and comfortably draw your shoulders back. Note how your chest is raised and ready to be filled with air. Again, draw a deep breath and say "ah." Now your lungs are filled with life-giving air, and your voice produces a strong, vibrant sound. Another exercise for establishing good posture for breathing and speaking is to lie flat on your back on the floor. Note how gravity pulls your shoulders back and how the flatness of the floor forces you into perfect posture. Again, your chest is raised and poised for receiving a full breath. Breathe deeply in this posture and you will see how refreshing a full dose of air can be for energizing your body and preparing your voice to speak. Lying flat on the floor also emphasizes the second physical element of good breathing—muscle control.

The Abdominal Muscles. Most voice and communication teachers teach breath control by emphasizing the use of the diaphragm, a large, horizontal, hidden muscle in the center of the torso. It is immediately beneath the lungs and separates the chest cavity from the organs below. Indeed, the diaphragm is central to breathing correctly, but it is not a muscle that can be observed or moved on command. Most people do not know how to move their diaphragm, even though they do it each time they breathe. But we can observe another key muscle group, and this is the one to concentrate on for good breath control.

Return to the floor exercise. As you lie flat on the floor, note how every breath occurs with the gentle rising and falling of the *abdominal muscles.* In this posture, there is no other way to breathe. To prove this, place a heavy book or object on your stomach. (If there is a young child in your house, have him or her sit gently on your stomach.) Suddenly, you lose your breath because the weight upon your abdomen has restricted the muscles that pump the air in and out of your lungs. As soon as the weight is moved off, your breath returns. As you lie on the floor, note which muscle movements bring air into your lungs and which cause you to exhale. Contrary to most people's expectation, it is the extension *outward* of the abdominal muscles that draws breath inward; and exhalation is caused when the muscles are drawn *inward.* Think of these muscles as part of a pump system. When they extend, the diaphragm is correspondingly drawn downward (toward your feet). This in turn causes the lungs to expand and draw air in through the mouth and nose. When the abdominal muscles are drawn inward, this forces the diaphragm up; the lungs compress, and air is pushed out. Keeping this pumping action in mind, try the following exercises in order to practice good breath control for public speaking.

1. Stand erect with good posture. Keep your shoulders comfortably back. Place your hands lightly on your stomach. As you take several deep breaths, feel the movements of your abdominal muscles. Note that they move out for inhalation and in for exhalation. (Do not take too many deep breaths at one time or dizziness may occur from hyperventilation.)

2. In the same posture, draw a deep breath and say "ah" using a moderate volume. Hold the vowel sound as long as you have breath. Try the exercise repeatedly and see if you can increase the length of time you hold the sound by gently restricting the inward movement of your abdominal muscles. This tension between exhaling and restricting your muscles to control the airflow is called breath control. It is used by singers and other people trained to put their voices to public use.

3. Stand with good posture, take deep breaths, and speak these vocal exercises:

    (a) "Ha, ha, ha, ha." Repeat, speaking more softly, more loudly, more gently, and more sharply.

    (b) Say the alphabet. Try doing it on one breath. Do not rush; speak each letter clearly. Now try saying the alphabet twice on one breath.

    (c) Say "ah" and hold the sound. Begin softly and gradually get louder, then softer. Try to go from very soft to very loud and back to very soft on a single breath. Repeat the exercise and see both how softly you can make the sound and how loudly you can make it, without becoming shrill or harsh.

4. For teaching purposes, in striving for good breath control it may be useful to see what it feels like when you do the opposite of what you desire. Try this exercise for making a breathy sound.

Take a deep breath, then speak and hold (sustain) the syllable
"ha." As you say it, continue to let extra air escape from your
lungs past your vocal cords. This mixes a bit of the "h" sound
into the "a" sound as you vocalize it. Note how airy the sound is.
See also how quickly your breath expires. The reason is that
much more air is being expelled than is needed for the sound.

> (a) Try reading the following line with this breathy sound,
> and note how this type of sound does not allow for good
> projection of the voice: "My, oh my, my voice is
> breathy."
>
> (b) Now try to do the opposite: speak with good breath con-
> trol. Remember to balance the abdominal muscles' nat-
> ural contraction inward with slight outward resistance
> in order to create the proper tension between exhala-
> tion and breath reservation. As you speak, elongate and
> let sing the vowel sounds in the following sentence:
> "Now my voice is strong and bold."

THE VOICE

The human voice is a remarkable instrument. The sound of
speech begins in the voice box (larynx). The vocal cords or folds
are simple vibrating membranes that make a small, twangy sound
when air is passed between them. But as that sound moves
upward into the air cavities of the throat and head, the sound
grows. It gains volume, strength, shape, and size through natural
human resonance. It also resonates through the bones and muscle mass of the speaker. When vocal sound is heard, it does not
resemble the small tone that it began as. It takes on the shape of
particular vowels, has personal character, is capable of carrying
long distances, and is almost infinitely variable as to tone and
volume. Learning to control the voice for use in public speaking
is crucial. Naturally, most people learn to speak well long before
they give any thought to speaking or reading in public. But there

are some fundamental things to keep in mind as one prepares to use his or her voice in embodying God's Word.

The first thing the speaker needs to remember is that the voice carries its sound mostly through the creation of vowel sounds. Try vocalizing on an "ee" or an "oh" sound. This is natural and easy to do. Next, try vocalizing on a "t" or a "p." Note how it is impossible to sustain the sound on these kinds of consonants. Now, try vocalizing on an "m" or an "l." See how these consonants *are* capable of sustaining vocal sound? They are called *voiced* consonants. When we hum, we are sustaining vocalization on the voiced consonant "m." Because the *nonvoiced* consonants cannot sustain vocalization, they merely add definition to the sounds we make. The effective reader will learn to let his or her voice carry on the vowel sounds of a text and use the consonants to bring clarity and articulation.

Second, volume is an important consideration for the lector. Most public speaking is done in the middle of a person's volume range. But the more emotive qualities of the voice are associated with the higher and lower extremes of the range. Speaking loudly can suggest great emphasis or passion. Speaking in a whisper can suggest fear or tenderness. Both are powerful elements of human speech and should be part of the reader's assortment of techniques.

A third vocal consideration is pitch. Here again, most of us speak in our middle range of pitch. Naturally, this varies as to gender, age, and vocal personality. Use of a broad range of pitch is another useful technique for making a Scripture reading come alive. If a reader simply applies the same range of inflection that is used in normal animated conversation, the reading will have vitality. These last two elements of vocal production, volume and pitch, are also related to the techniques of oral interpretation. Here we are concerned with understanding what the voice is doing. In the final chapter we will consider volume and pitch, along with other oral interpretation techniques, and demonstrate how they can be employed for good effect in making a text come alive.

In summary, the voice can be used effectively in reading as the lector learns to attend to these things:

1. Do not swallow vowels or let them trail off. Let the vowels carry the words.

2. Allow the voice to resonate on elongated vowel sounds for greater emphasis of certain words, or when greater volume or projection is desired. Also, elongate the vowels in a phrase when a smooth effect is desired, such as in reading poetic elements of a text. Skillful use of vowels can allow phrases to sing, if that is the desired effect.

3. Use the voiced consonant sounds (such as l, m, n, ng, r, v, w, y, and z) to string words in a phrase together. As the reader moves from vowels to voiced consonants, the sound does not break and a seamless phrase occurs.

4. Be careful to avoid the bad habit of everyday speech where consonants are elided or eliminated. For example, say "coming" rather than "comin'."

5. Stress the nonvoiced consonants in a line of text when action is suggested. Let the consonants serve percussively to create energy and tension.

6. Use the careful pronunciation of vowels and consonants as a way to regulate the pace of speech. It is difficult to speak too quickly when the reader allows for each sound to be properly articulated.

7. Pay attention to the pitch applied to vowel sounds, especially at the ends of sentences. Try to avoid the habit of letting the pitch drop or rise regularly as sentences conclude. Pitch should not fall into predictable patterns, but be matched to the movement and meaning of the phrase. Also, watch for the singsong pattern that occurs when the pitch rises and falls regularly and repeatedly.

8. Vary pace and pitch according to the sense of the phrase. Avoid using only the middle range of your voice for long sections. Try to bring the animation of a casual conversation into the reading.

9. Remember to speak loudly and distinctly enough for *all* to hear. The ultimate goal is communication. If the reader's words cannot be made out by those in the back row or by

those with hearing problems, the reader is not achieving his or her purpose.

10. Always practice reading aloud. Lines of text can be trickier to pronounce than they look. Do not presume that reading silently is a suitable substitute for vocalizing the text.

Finally, the person learning to use his or her voice effectively in public reading should learn to exaggerate his or her effort in order to achieve the desired outcome.

Imagine this scene: A group of high school students has been recruited to assist with worship on Sunday. They gather on Saturday morning to practice. When the student assigned to read the lessons steps up to the lectern to practice her readings, the others sit in the pews to provide feedback. The student begins. Before long she is interrupted by her peers. "Slow down. You're reading too fast," someone tells her. She pauses, mentally adjusts the tempo of her reading, and begins again. But she is interrupted a second time. "No, we said to slow down! We still can't make out what you are saying."

What is happening in this common situation? It is a rule of performance that what is perceived as a suitable adjustment from the internal perspective of the performer is measured differently from the objective perspective of the audience. The performer needs to exaggerate her adjustment internally in order for it to be perceived as correct externally. As our young reader continues to practice the pacing of her reading, her friends guide her until she achieves a good general pace. In the end, it may seem to her that she is speaking far too slowly, but the listeners will assure her that the pace is just right. This law of performance is true not only for youthful readers of Scripture but also for more mature lectors. Learning to judge our work objectively is critical; we learn such judgment through the honest feedback of peers who will help us to balance internal perceptions against external observations.

What follows is a set of exercises that will assist the lector in learning to control the voice and in acquiring skill in the use of vocal techniques. The exercises should be performed with good posture and breath control. Try them in private practice as well as in small groups.

1. Speak these exercises. Repeat them, focusing on the elements of vocal production that are suggested with each.
   (a) "Mah, may, mee, moh, moo." Make each repetition smooth and seamless. Let the "m" sounds connect the syllables to allow them to produce a single, unbroken phrase.
   (b) Speak the same syllabic phrase with the following emphases of pitch: rising, as in a question; falling, as if in sadness; rising and falling, as to emphasize the middle syllable "mee."
   (c) Repeat the syllabic phrase, experimenting with volume. Speak it moderately, more softly, loudly, shout it, whisper it. Try speaking it with changing volume, going from soft to loud and from loud to soft.
   (d) Read aloud the following verse. Emphasize the consonants. Make them crisp and sharply articulated to suggest energy, passion, and tension: "Is it not written, 'My house shall be called a house of prayer for all the nations'? But you have made it a den of robbers" (Mark 11:17).

2. Speak the following lines, emphasizing the vowel sounds. Elongate the vowel patterns and emphasize the voiced consonants to let the phrases sing.
   (a) "Four score and seven years ago, our Fathers brought forth upon this continent a new nation, conceived in liberty" (from the Gettysburg Address, Abraham Lincoln).
   (b) "How could we sing the Lord's song in a foreign land?" (Psalm 137:4).
   (c) "When autumn cools and youth is cold, when limbs their heavy harvest hold" (from "O Blessed Spring," a hymn by Susan Palo Cherwien).

3. Speak the following line in two ways. First, emphasize the vowel sounds to make the sentence smooth and musical. Second, emphasize the consonant sounds to fill the sentence with energy and tension. If in a group, discuss which version seems most appropriate to the text, or what combination of effects might be used.

"Wail, for the day of the LORD is near; it will come like destruction from the Almighty" (Isaiah 13:6).

4. Speak the following sentence, placing an emphasis (in volume and pitch) on the italicized word. Repeat the exercise, changing emphasis as indicated. Note (and describe) the change in meaning that occurs as the emphasis shifts.

"*I* do not know the man."

"I do *not* know the man."

"I do not *know* the man."

"I do not know the *man*."

5. Have two people in the group engage in conversation while the others listen. Have one person relate an exciting event (such as a concert, sporting event, or party that he or she has attended), while the second person asks questions and shares natural responses. While they speak, the listeners should note the natural enthusiasm that fuels the conversation. Afterward, discuss the range of pitch, energy, and pace that was demonstrated in the conversation. Also, discuss how to bring that level of animation into the reading of Scripture.

THE EYES

"Take off your glasses," she said.

"What?" I replied in panic.

"Take off your glasses so they can see your eyes." It was my college voice teacher. She had accompanied me to a contest in which I was to sing an aria. I did not need my glasses to read my music; that was memorized and well prepared. I needed my glasses to find the piano—and my place on stage. Afterward, I needed them to find a safe place to hide after botching my solo. My teacher knew that the eyes communicate almost as much as the voice does. She wanted the judges to see my eyes and find in them the *amor* I was singing about in Italian. What they saw, I am certain, was angst, much the same look that some lectors have when they present a lesson that has not been properly prepared.

The eyes are powerful tools for communication. They are used at the lectern not merely for reading the words of the appointed text but to add meaning to the oral interpretation of Scripture. This is done in three ways. The most obvious is to use them in looking at the people who listen to the reading. The second is to add gesture. Eyes do sparkle, smile, or show fear and other emotions. Third, the eyes can serve as mirrors of a speaker's thought. The second of these aspects of eye communication will be addressed in the final section of this chapter when we consider additional forms of facial expression. But here our purpose will be to suggest how a well-prepared reader can make effective use of the eyes in two ways: in looking at the audience and in letting the audience see what the reader sees in his or her imagination.

Eye contact. It is generally understood that the reader should maintain some level of eye contact with the audience. It cannot be constant unless the lesson has been committed to memory. Even then, it would ring false if the speaker looked only at the faces of those in the audience; that is not how we communicate in casual conversation. Typically, we look only for a moment at our conversation partner when speaking. Then we look away to focus our thoughts or to ponder an image. At times our eyes are drawn in the direction of some nearby movement. Then we might look back at our listener. In reading Scripture, we practice to be more focused than that. Still, just as in conversation, eye contact with the listeners should only be occasional. The audience understands that the reader is not reciting. This does not mean, however, that the reading should be done carelessly. In some cases, it might be better for a reader to avoid looking up at all than to do so mechanically, ineptly, or in a bouncing manner.

Looking at the audience during a reading serves another good purpose. It helps one to know if he or she is communicating effectively. If the reader sees that people are straining to hear words or to understand diction, he or she can make adjustments in delivery to solve the problem.

The guide for planning when to seek eye contact with the audience is the text. If one is relating a story, it makes sense to look at the listeners occasionally. Here the reader does so at those points in the story where a line needs to be underscored. Think of looking up at these points as the performative equivalent of highlighting a text with a fluorescent marker. For example, one might read:

> [looking at the text] They went to him and woke him up, shouting, "Master, Master, we are perishing!" And he woke up and rebuked the wind and the raging waves; they ceased, and there was a calm. He said to them, [looking at the audience] "Where is your faith?" (Luke 8:24-25)

If one is reading a psalmist's prayer, it would make just as much literary sense to refrain from looking up as it does when one is praying other forms of prayer. When the lesson is from the Epistles, the key is to identify once again those places in the text that can best be underscored by a definite look directly at the audience. For example:

> [looking at the text] So if you have been raised with Christ, seek the things that are above, where Christ is, seated at the right hand of God. [looking at the audience] Set your minds on things that are above, not on things that are on earth. (Colossians 3:1-2)

Remember not to overdo looking at the audience when reading a text. The time to make eye contact is when it makes the text more clear, or underscores some element in the text that can use visual emphasis. Charles Bartow summarized the point nicely in *Effective Speech Communication in Leading Worship*

(Abingdon Press, 1988). He said, "*Quality* of eye contact is more important than *quantity* of eye contact" (p. 103).

Effective use of eye contact presupposes careful preparation and practice on the part of the lector. After studying the text and determining how to interpret it, the reader needs to mark or highlight those places where he or she intends to look at the audience. Sufficient practice is then needed so as to deliver these critical lines without error. The whole purpose of highlighting a phrase is ruined if the text itself is misspoken.

The Eyes as Mirrors. The other purpose for looking up from the text has to do with allowing the eyes to mirror the reader's thought. When this happens, the reader does not look at the audience, but looks up and off at some imagined object. Imagine, for example, if someone is speaking to you about her grandmother. She pauses, smiles, and looks off at the wall or a point in space. It is clear to you that in the speaker's imagination she is seeing her grandmother. But you do not look off to that same spot on the wall or in the air to find the image of her grandmother. You keep your eyes on the *speaker's* eyes and see in them what she sees in her imagination. Her eyes are the mirrors through which you envision what she imagines.

The same effect can take place in reading Scripture. When the text calls for it, the reader might look off the page and away from the direct gaze of the listeners to a neutral point in space as a way to cast an image from the text that is worth pondering. The listener is then drawn into reflection of the object of the reader's consideration. Suppose, for example, the reader were to read Jesus' lament over Jerusalem from Matthew 23:37. How appropriate it would be to glance off toward an imaginary city when he or she speaks the words, "Jerusalem, Jerusalem, the city that kills the prophets and stones those who are sent to it!" Here again, any line delivered with eyes removed from the text must be well rehearsed so that the reader does not spoil the effect by hurriedly glancing back at the text in the midst of the climactic line. The following are exercises designed to get the learner thinking about how and when to use eye contact in Scripture reading.

1. Practice reading the following passages, looking up at the audience while delivering the underlined words.

(a) Then David slept with his ancestors, and was buried in the city of David. <u>The time that David reigned over Israel was forty years;</u> he reigned seven years in Hebron, and thirty-three years in Jerusalem. So Solomon sat on the throne of his father David; and his kingdom was firmly established. (1 Kings 2:10-12)

(b) And just then some people were carrying a paralyzed man lying on a bed. When Jesus saw their faith, he said to the paralytic, <u>"Take heart, son; your sins are forgiven."</u> Then some of the scribes said to themselves, <u>"This man is blaspheming."</u> But Jesus, perceiving their thoughts, said, "Why do you think evil in your hearts? For which is easier, to say, 'Your sins are forgiven,' or to say, 'Stand up and walk'? But so that you may know that the Son of Man has authority on earth to forgive sins"—he then said to the paralytic—<u>"Stand up, take your bed and go to your home."</u> (Matthew 9:2-6)

2. Practice reading from the parables of Jesus. Photocopy the text, or type it so that you can experiment with different ways to mark the text for eye contact. Read the parable several times, selecting different lines to emphasize with audience eye contact. Ask members of your training group to help identify which emphases seem to be most effective. Discuss with the group how to determine which phrases to emphasize.

3. Read the following passage aloud (Matthew 23:37-38). Each time experiment with indirect eye contact by looking off the page and away from your audience while delivering the words in bold print. Discuss which version seems most effective.

(a) **"Jerusalem, Jerusalem, the city that kills the prophets and stones those who are sent to it!** How often have I desired to gather your children together as a hen gathers her brood under her wings, and you were not willing! See, your house is left to you, desolate."

(b) "Jerusalem, Jerusalem, the city that kills the prophets and stones those who are sent to it! **How often have I desired to gather your children together as a hen gathers her brood under her wings,** and you were not willing! See, your house is left to you, desolate."

(c) "Jerusalem, Jerusalem, the city that kills the prophets and stones those who are sent to it! How often have I desired to gather your children together as a hen gathers her brood under her wings, and you were not willing! **See, your house is left to you, desolate.**"

4. Read the following passage. Follow this key for practicing eye contact: when the words are underlined, look at the audience; when the words are in bold, look up and away from the audience.

Be patient, therefore, beloved, until the coming of the Lord. The farmer waits for the precious crop from the earth, being patient with it until it receives the early and the late rains. <u>You also must be patient.</u> Strengthen your hearts, for the coming of the Lord is near. Beloved, do not grumble against one another, so that you may not be judged. **See, the Judge is standing at the doors!** (James 5:7-9)

GESTURE

In this chapter, gesture is presented in its broadest sense, that of using body movement to bring meaning or add emphasis to Scripture readings. Of course the use of hand gestures comes first to mind. In everyday speech, it is common to gesticulate with hands and arms, extending them for emphasis, sculpting the air in imaginary statues of thought, and so on. Nowadays one can readily see the natural tie of human speech to hand gesture by watching people talk on cell phones. It can be amusing to observe the physical affirmation of these people as they speak to unseen listeners. But this familiar type of gesture may be the *least* useful for public reading of Scripture. Imagine how awkward it would look to see a lector performing sweeping hand gestures while keeping his or her eyes fixed on the words of the text. Even if the reader coordinated his or her hand movements with glances at the audience, the gestures would appear unnatural and contrived. As a general rule, hand gestures are seldom useful in Scripture reading. However, one well-known speech teacher at Princeton Theological Seminary described an instance in which the use of a simple hand gesture *was* applied with stunning effect. G. Robert Jacks recounts in his book, *Getting the Word Across: Speech Communication for Pastors and Lay Leaders* (Eerdmans, 1995):

> This was during a chapel service years ago, when . . . Dean Elmer Homrighausen was reading from Acts, chapter 26. Dean Homrighausen (everyone called him "Homey") was a marvelously expressive person to begin with, and this exuberance naturally carried over into his reading of Scripture, which was always electric. These were the words he was reading:
> And Agrippa said to Paul, "In a short time you think to make me a Christian!"
> And Paul said, "Whether short or long, I would to God that not only you but also all who hear me this day might become such as I am . . ."
> and then the Dean looked up, paused, held his fists out, wrists together, and finished:
> ". . . —except for these chains." (pp. 41-42)

In this instance, the technique was effective, partly because it came at the end of the reading and partly because of the stature and personality of the speaker.

Other kinds of gestures broaden the definition of the term and provide useful tools for the reader of Scripture. They include facial gesture, eye expression, and posture.

The face is remarkably expressive. Try this little exercise the next time you are watching a television program. Turn down the volume and try to determine the tone of the conversation or the mood of the speakers simply by watching their facial expressions. A surprising amount of information will reveal itself to you even if you cannot hear the speech. Keep this in mind when preparing to read a lesson in worship. People will be watching you and taking in information about the reading as they look at your face. Often the clearest piece of information conveyed by the face of an ill-prepared reader is that the Bible is boring.

Our goal as well-prepared readers is to let our face shine with appropriate expression. If we are engaged by the text, it should be reflected on our faces; and our expressions should reinforce the meaning of the reading. Some lessons call for sincerity, others for exuberance. Some are joyful, others somber. The range of emotion associated with a text is not hard to capture. It is matched by the natural range of expression that is available to any speaker. Here, as with other techniques, if the speaker simply learns to bring the kind of facial expression used in ordinary conversation into his or her reading, it will be just right. The average adult does not need to practice facial expression; it is a natural reaction to the world around us. Looks of surprise, horror, delight, and so forth, come to us as automatically as do chuckles or sighs. The careful lector will be aware that people are watching and will strive to use the face as a rhetorical tool for making the meaning of a lesson clear.

Well-prepared readers will also realize that there is no "down time" for facial gesture. The reader's facial expressions should move with the text and be appropriate to the changing mood throughout the reading. One way to allow the audience a clear view of one's face is to read the lessons from a moderately sized Bible. Practice holding the Bible high enough for it to be easy to see and comfortable to hold. Note how much more the face is elevated in comparison to when one reads from a text that is placed on the lectern. When holding the Bible, let it lie in a horizontal plane in your hands lest it block your face from the audience's view. Remember, the point here is to allow facial gesture throughout the reading to be part of the interpretive technique.

As mentioned above, an important part of facial gesture is eye expression. It would be impossible to separate the expressiveness of the eyes from the overall expression of the face. One could hardly have eyes that sparkle with mirth while the mouth is down-turned in sadness. The thing to remember about eye expressiveness is simply that they must be seen in order to allow the face's full expressiveness to shine forth. Poor lighting can cast shadows on the reader's eyes and give a false impression of what the face is saying. Also, lectors who wear glasses should be aware of their potential for obscuring the expressiveness of the eyes. Reflections of light against the lenses of glasses can be as concealing as wearing sunglasses. On the days they serve as lector, people who use contact lenses might make a point of wearing them.

As an exercise in facial gesture, play the following game of charades. Select from the following list of emotions. Using only your face, try to give a silent impression of the emotion. Have the other group members try to guess the emotion you are miming.

anger	amusement
pride	fear
terror	compassion
sternness	eagerness
understanding	consternation
love (as for a child)	romantic love
frustration	resignation
uncertainty	thoughtfulness
quiet joy	delirious joy
peace	hopefulness

The final element of gesture to be considered is posture. The way we stand or sit says a lot about what is on our minds. Knowing that the body interprets human moods gives the lector another useful tool for making a reading come alive. Generally, the reader should stand with good posture. This looks appropriate for the worship setting and it allows the reader to have good breath support. A reader who hunches over the lectern constricts lung expansion, lessens vocal capacity, restricts the audience's view of his or her face, and demonstrates a lack of vitality. A reader who looks sluggish will most likely sound sluggish.

Occasionally, a reader may want to vary his or her posture in order to bring out the meaning of a text. One might stand especially erect to register a quality of surprise, confidence, or inflexibility. Or, one might stoop slightly to embody an attitude of prayer, humility, weariness, or despair. As a lector prepares his or her reading, speaking the text aloud will help to determine which facial and body expressions will be most fitting. In your training group discuss the various attitudes of posture that can be useful as tools for oral interpretation.

As part of your private practice or in working as a group, go into the chancel of your church and practice standing at the lectern. For placement of the hands, try resting them lightly on the sides of the lectern. This looks natural and allows for unobtrusive page turns, as they are needed. Or, you may choose to use one hand to keep your place on the page of text. Take note of your height in comparison to the size of the podium. Check to see if it is adjustable. Try to place your text about chest level. Any lower and the audience will see primarily the top of your head. This also makes it difficult when you look up, because your head will appear to bob as you deal with the wide angle between where your text is placed and your view of the audience. Putting the text any higher than mid-chest level can block the audience's view of your face. If your lectern is not adjustable, experiment with where you place your text on the podium. Tall people will want to move it up and out toward the audience; this raises the head. Short people will want to move the text in close to bring the chin down to a comfortable level.

As suggested earlier, it is also good to practice reading from a Bible held in your hands. When reading without a lectern, try to avoid reading your lesson from a piece of paper or bulletin insert. It looks better to hold a Bible and to place, if necessary, a page with your marked text in it. This gives the proper impression that the Word of God is substantial and that it is not disposable like a paper hamburger wrapping.

The techniques and suggestions contained in this chapter have been designed to aid the lector in learning to use the body in presentation of the scriptural text. Body control enables the lector to achieve success in the use of oral interpretation techniques, which will be the subject of the chapter that follows.

Chapter 5

TECHNIQUES FOR ORAL
INTERPRETATION OF SCRIPTURE

This simple and external demonstration of the divine word ought, indeed, to be fully sufficient for the production of faith, if it were not obstructed by our blindness and perverseness. But such is our propensity to error, that our mind can never adhere to divine truth; such is our dullness, that we can never discern the light of it. Therefore nothing is effected by the word, without illumination of the Holy Spirit.

—John Calvin, *Institutes of the Christian Religion*

Calvin has a rather low view of human capacity for comprehending God's Word. He is, nonetheless, correct. How can the human mind wrap itself around the great mysteries of our faith without assistance? If we achieve any understanding of divine things, it is because of the Holy Spirit who, as Luther says, calls, gathers, and enlightens us.

God finds many ways to inspire us to faith and enlighten us through the Word. Our task in this book has been to consider the various ways that the Holy Spirit can use us in service of this holy process of faith development. In the first chapter we explored the ways that God calls and equips lectors for their work. We learned that to be an effective tool of the Spirit requires prayer and reliance upon God's gifts. In chapter 2 we considered the theological significance of the task before us. Serving as a reader in worship is worth our finest efforts because we are nothing less than spokespersons for God. Chapter 3 proposed that the successful lector will be a student of the Bible who, by virtue of careful study, is prepared to deliver an appropriate interpretation of a scriptural text. The focus of the previous chapter was on the use of the body in making readings come alive. In this final chapter we turn to the consideration of certain technical aspects of oral interpretation such as phrasing, rate of speech, and word emphasis. These, too, aid us in becoming useful tools of the Spirit in making the Word heard and understood.

This book is just one resource among many available to help lectors acquire skills for their work. The subject of this chapter alone is the topic of entire texts on the public reading of Scripture. Our intention here has been to provide an introductory volume that gives guidance to those considering this ministry in their congregations and to provide them with some *basic* skills to get started. For further study, the reader is directed to the annotated bibliography found in appendix B. (Remember from the first chapter, that a commitment to continuing education is one of the qualifications for people who choose to accept this ministry.)

In a fairly brief manner, this chapter will examine a list of six interpretive categories. These items are handled differently by various writers. For example, the first four (rate, pitch or inflection, volume, and pause) are treated as elements of "vocalics" by Jana Childers in *Performing the Word: Preaching as Theatre*, while Charles Bartow identifies some of them (pause and inflection) as elements of "emphasis" in *Effective Speech Communication in Leading Worship*. I will isolate the terms and offer guidance as to their use, regardless of classification. A few exercises for private and group practice will accompany each item. The six categories to be considered are *rate of delivery, pitch or inflection, volume, pause, phrasing,* and *emphasis.*

RATE OF DELIVERY

One of the first things to determine in thinking about presenting a text is the rate at which to deliver it. Some texts should be read slowly, meditatively. Others are filled with action and want for a quicker delivery. The text will guide in this matter. Listen to it. Move with it. Look for the action words and let them suggest how to proceed. In determining the rate of speech, remember these two things: First, use variety. Any steady paced reading will become predictable and uninteresting. Second, practice matching the perception of pace with that of the listeners. As suggested in the last chapter, what seems slow to the reader may not seem slow to the audience. For practice in determining the right pace for a reading, continue to work with a study group and receive feedback on all the oral exercises performed. Readers assist one another when each person is open to giving and receiving honest critique.

Here is another exercise one can do alone: *tape record reading a passage at different rates. Range from reading too quickly to what one thinks is far too slowly. Listen to the tape and make an objective determination about which version best presents the movement of the text. Then read the text again, reciting it along with the taped version that seems correct. Try to get an internal feel for the pacing that seems objectively appropriate.*

PITCH OR INFLECTION

In the last chapter I spoke about the pitch of a speaker's voice and how it varies, depending on age, gender, and other circumstances. Even the time of day can make a difference. Early in the morning, voices are usually significantly lower than later in the day when they are well warmed through use. The general pitch of a reader's voice should be natural and comfortable. It will sound odd (and can eventually do some harm) if a reader tries to speak above or below his or her natural pitch. In normal conversation, we tend to use a fairly wide range of pitch. We inflect our voices upward or downward to add meaning to our words. If we speak a phrase with a rising tone (/) at the end, it suggests uncertainty, lack of completion, or that we are asking a question. If we speak with a falling tone (\ ) at the end, it suggests finality or certainty. Consider this example: "You don't mean that, do you?" Speak it with a rising tone: "You don't mean that, do you /?" Note how the question sounds like it requires an answer. The response could be yes or no and either would make sense. Now speak the sentence with a falling tone: "You don't mean that, do you \?" Now it appears that the speaker is certain about it. The question seems rhetorical and the answer is probably no.

The other kind of inflection in speech is the circumflex (or combination). We can go up in pitch, then down (/ \ ) on a word or phrase. Or, we can go down, then up (\ /). Circumflex inflections suggest complex thoughts like wonder or suspicion. For example, say the phrase, "Wait a minute" with a rising and falling tone: "/ Wait a minute \ ." Notice how it sounds like something fishy is going on?

For practice in using and understanding inflections, try speaking the following lines from the psalms and note how the meaning changes as the inflections change. Try this alone and in a small group. Discuss the range of meaning implied as each type of inflection is used.

1. Psalm 3:1
   (a) O Lord, how many are my foes / !

   (b) O Lord, how many are my foes \ !

2. Psalm 18:4
   (a) The cords of death encompassed me /;
       the torrents of perdition assailed me /;
       the cords of Sheol entangled me /;
       the snares of death confronted me \ .

(b) The cords of death encompassed me \ ;
the torrents of perdition assailed me \ ;
the cords of Sheol entangled me \ ;
the snares of death confronted me \ .

3. Psalm 76:1
(a) In Judah God is known /,
his name is great in Israel \ .

(b) In Judah God is known \ ,
his name is great in Israel \ .

(c) / In Judah God is known \ ,
/ his name is great in Israel \ .

VOLUME

Whether persons tend to be soft-spoken, moderate, or loud in speech volume, they can learn to adjust their volume to suit the needs of textual interpretation. Just as with rate of speech, the key is to use variety throughout a reading to keep it interesting. The text will usually indicate where more energy should be added. Again, move with the text. When reading action scenes, a quicker pace and louder volume makes sense. When reading something prayerful or meditative, a slower pace and lower volume would be appropriate. As the focus or perspective changes within a reading, the volume might change along with rate and energy.

Volume can be used in a reading to add interest and emphasis. There might be a certain line in a text that begs to be spoken loudly. Another line might be more powerfully delivered if whispered. I recall how effective it was on one occasion, when, during a reading of the passion narrative, the lector shouted the words "I do not know the man!" He did this as he voiced Peter's *third* betrayal of Jesus. It was unexpected and significantly louder than the first and second betrayal statements. But it was just right. Yes, the listener knew, this was the level of fear to which Peter had been pushed. Several verses later, when the reader whispered the words, "And he went out and wept bitterly," every listener knew why.

The foregoing example was dramatic largely because the reader was willing to use as wide a range of volume as necessary. But such extremes are appropriate only in special circumstances. Usually, the speaker should aim for a range of volume that is similar to that used in normal conversation. The key is to employ a fluid range of volume to bring out the meaning of a text.

Most congregations today use public address systems to assist speakers and to ensure that their words are heard. Be sure to spend some practice time with the system the congregation uses. But do not assume that electronic amplification will take care of volume concerns. The speaker varies his or her volume not only to be clearly heard but also to be expressive. Use of a microphone can actually increase the levels to which the speaker adjusts speech volume, rather than diminish them. For example, one might speak a key word or phrase more softly with a microphone than without. Without it, a whisper might well go unheard. With a microphone, one might lean in and use it to deliver a stunningly quiet expression.

For practice in achieving effective use of volume, follow the suggestions for reading the verses below. If it feels awkward to raise your voice as indicated, you may want to refer back to the discussion of abandonment in chapter 2.

1. Read this text in a moderate voice; at the last phrase, speak more loudly and emphatically.

Now if you are unwilling to serve the LORD, choose this day whom you will serve, whether the gods your ancestors served in the region beyond the River or the gods of the Amorites in whose land you are living; *but as for me and my household, we will serve the LORD.* (Joshua 24:15)

2. Speak these verses from the psalms several times, experimenting with volume. When you come to the italicized phrases, try for a contrasting volume level (that is, go from moderate to loud, or from loud to soft). Discuss in class which combination seems to be the most effective for each passage.

(a) He makes wars cease to the end of the earth;
    he breaks the bow, and shatters the spear;
    he burns the shields with fire.
  "Be still, and know that I am God!
    I am exalted among the nations,
    I am exalted in the earth." (Psalm 46:9-10)

(b) For forty years I loathed that generation
    and said, *"They are a people whose hearts go astray,*
    and they do not regard my ways."
  Therefore in my anger I swore,
    "They shall not enter my rest." (Psalm 95:10-11)

(c) In my distress I cry to the LORD,
    that he may answer me:
  "Deliver me, O LORD,
    from lying lips,
    from a deceitful tongue." (Psalm 120:1-2)

(d) I was glad when they said to me,
    "Let us go to the house of the LORD!"
  Our feet are standing
    within your gates,
    O Jerusalem. (Psalm 122:1-2)

3. Read the following passage in two ways. First, speak the italicized words loudly and harshly. Second, speak the italicized words quietly and intensely. Discuss with the group which reading feels the most appropriate and which delivers the key line with greater impact.

But when [John] saw many Pharisees and Sadducees coming for baptism, he said to them, *"You brood of vipers! Who warned you to flee from the wrath to come?"* (Matthew 3:7)

PAUSE

A pause is the speaker's friend. We often assume a long pause will be construed as a mistake. *"Oops,"* we think, *"the listeners are wondering if I have lost my place."* But that is rarely how the listener is using the pause. This is time for absorption of the material, and time to prepare for what is coming. The pause is not a hole in communication, but an important part of it. It is like the musical rest. The composer knows to build rests into musical lines in order to create proper phrasing and to give time for the musicians to breathe. Momentary silence is just as important for readers of Scripture.

Pauses do several things. First, they emphasize that which has gone before. The last thing the listeners hear before a pause is the first thing they are left to consider during it. Only when a pause is unduly long does the listener move from contemplation of the subject to wonder about the purpose of the pause. If the material is complex, longer pauses are appropriate to give listeners time to sort through the logic of the discourse. Second, pauses prepare the listener for what is to come. When subjects or moods change and the reader does not provide a timely pause, the listener will expect that the subject or mood is continuing along as before. An unexpected pause can set words and phrases off for emphasis. Consider, for example, this line: "Her name was Elizabeth." Speak it with a short pause before the name, like this: "Her name was | Elizabeth." This gives the sense that the speaker needs a moment to remember the person's name. Now speak it with a long pause before the name: "Her name was | | Elizabeth." See how this heightens the tension about the name. One gets the sense that there is something very interesting about this particular name. Pauses are also used for shaping phrases and giving the reader time to breathe. Because pausing is closely related to phrasing, the exercises for practicing pauses will be offered following the next section.

PHRASING

All verbal communication comes in manageable units of thought known as phrases. Phrases are manageable because they can be delivered on a single breath and because they present one idea at a time. A sentence might consist of a single phrase. Or a reader might break a long sentence into two or more phrases. The ear identifies the phrase by the pauses that precede and follow it. The trick for the reader (and it can be tricky!) is to determine how to organize material into phrases that make the most sense. This requires careful preparation and experimentation. The meaning of some passages can be completely changed if the phrasing is off. Consider the following example. It is such a humorous example that it is included in nearly every book on oral interpretation of Scripture. Here it is again. The passage from Luke 2:16 tells what happened when the shepherds followed the angel's suggestion to go to Bethlehem to see the newborn king: "They went with haste and found Mary and Joseph, and the child lying in the manger." The image becomes funny when one reads the verse aloud giving a single, slight pause after the word "haste": "They went with haste | and found Mary and Joseph, and the child lying in the manger." As a person who grew up on a farm, I spent plenty of time stuffing hay into mangers. But I never saw one large enough to accommodate *three people*. Clearly, a pause needs to be placed after "Mary and Joseph": "They went with haste | and found Mary and Joseph, | | and the child lying in a manger."

Did you notice that the example only became humorous when you captured the picture in your imagination? That gives us a clue for determining how to fashion good phrases out of textual cloth. Try to visualize what you are speaking about. As you begin your practice with a text, let the words build up images in your mind. Then work at crafting phrases so as to make single, sensible images.

In the following example, see how the first phrasing of Isaiah 30:32 casts a confusing set of images, whereas the second seems to project things clearly.

1. And every stroke of the staff of punishment | that the Lord lays upon him will be | to the sound of timbrels and lyres; | | battling with brandished | arm he will fight him.

2. And every stroke of the staff of punishment that the Lord lays upon him | will be to the sound of timbrels and lyres; | | battling with brandished arm [God] will fight him.

In turning textual phrases, we figure out precisely where to place pauses. This, as suggested above, can be tricky. Why? Because our temptation is to phrase at punctuation marks. Sometimes this *is* the correct way to bring out the sense of a text. But often a pause is needed where there is no punctuation mark. And, in many instances, pausing at a comma will misrepresent the meaning of a text. Consider the following examples. As you read the first set aloud, note how a pause at the comma seems to work properly in bringing forth the meaning of the text.

1. Then I turned to see whose voice it was that spoke to me, | | and on turning I saw seven golden lampstands, | and in the midst of the lampstands I saw one like the Son of Man, | clothed with a long robe and with a golden sash across his chest. (Revelation 1:12-13)

2. If you are confident that you belong to Christ, | remind yourself of this, | that just as you belong to Christ, | so also do we." (2 Corinthians 10:7*b*)

The next example is one of Paul's long-winded sentences. If you read it as marked by the punctuation, you might pass out from lack of oxygen before you reach the first comma. Read it aloud and pause in the places marked. (Do not give in to the temptation to pause at all of the commas that occur in the end of the passage.) As you read, notice how the sense of the passage is made clear by pausing in places where there is no punctuation. Now read the passage a second time, pausing both where indicated *and* wherever there is a comma. See how this chops up the flow of the passage and separates ideas that ought to be joined.

> But if you call yourself a Jew | | and rely on the law and boast of your relation to God | and know his will and determine what is best because you are instructed in the law, | | and if you are sure that you are a guide to the blind, a light to those who are in darkness, | a corrector of the foolish, a teacher of children, | having in the law the embodiment of knowledge and truth, | | you, then, that teach others, | | will you not teach yourself? (Romans 2:17-21*a*)

Here are two more suggestions for calculating where to place pauses for proper phrasing. The first has to do with words that introduce quotations. The general rule of thumb (and take special note here because this goes against our natural inclination) is *not* to pause after these kinds of words.

Consider this example from the story of the Last Supper in Luke 22:19: "Then [Jesus] took a loaf of bread, and when he had given thanks, he broke it and gave it to them, saying, 'This is my body, which is given for you. Do this in remembrance of me.'" The natural urge is to pause at the commas. This might be right for the first comma. I would not pause at the second. But the third and fourth commas are problematic. If the reader pauses at both of them, he or she has now set the word "saying" off with great emphasis. In the meaning of the phrase, however, it offers nothing. It is merely an audible way to put the saying in quotation marks. The word should be invisible, or unnoticeable. The way to do that is to make it a springboard into the quotation by *avoiding a pause after it.* Speak the phrase aloud in this manner: "and gave it to them, | | saying This is my body. . . ." See how the word "saying" disappears as the quotation begins.

Verbal quotation marks are sometimes represented by the words "and said." Note in the following example from Matthew 26:49 how they need to receive the same treatment: "At once [Judas] came up to Jesus and said, 'Greetings, Rabbi!' " Read it aloud twice. First, read it with a pause after "and said." Next, read it with a single strong pause after the word "Jesus." See how the second reading presents the proper phrasing and how it heightens the tension at the moment when these two friends meet? The kind of pause that is appropriate in this instance is often referred to by the overused phrase "pregnant pause." The cliché is accurate in this case, however, because a strong pause here suggests that something important is about to be delivered. And so it is—a betrayal.

The second phrasing suggestion relates to words of address (technically known as vocatives). The guideline here is to avoid pausing *before* such words. Remember, the pause emphasizes that which goes before. But it is the person or thing being addressed that needs emphasis. For example, if one said, "Come, | my friends," the emphasis is on coming rather than on who it is that should come. Instead, one would say "Come, my friends" without a pause. Try reading the following passage from Psalm 84:8-9, pausing only at the places indicated:

"O LORD God of Hosts, | hear my prayer; | | give ear, O God of Jacob! | | Behold our shield, O God; | | look on the face of your anointed."

In a small group, try reading the passage with pauses before the words of address merely for comparison. Discuss the difference with the group.

Phrasing largely has to do with how we use the pause. Another category that relies upon the pause is emphasis.

EMPHASIS

In every discourse, some words need emphasis to lift them up and indicate their relative importance to other words. Their importance depends on the speaker's intention. In an earlier exercise, you practiced saying "I do not know the man." If you emphasize the "I," the meaning is that, though some may know him, you do not. If you emphasize "man," you suggest that you might know a particular woman or child, but that you do not know this man.

One way to emphasize a word or phrase is to wrap it in pauses. In *How to Read the Bible Aloud*, Jack Rang offers this provocative example. He is reporting on a reading of the story of Daniel by the great actor Charles Laughton. Although there are no markings in the text to cue him, Laughton paints a picture of disdain for the Jews held by the person in the story who complains to the king: "There are certain Jews whom you have set over the affairs of the province. . . ." He accomplishes this by placing a pause before *and* after the word "Jews." Like this: "There are certain | | Jews | | | whom you have. . . ." See how the line now drips with disgust due to the emphasis of the word?

Emphasis can also be added by using combinations of effects such as volume, inflection, and stress. Practice privately and in a group the following exercise. Discuss how the meaning changes as you try different ways of emphasizing the italicized word.

1. Speak the italicized word more loudly, with a rising pitch (/):
   What are we having for *dinner* /? What are *we* / having for dinner? *What* / are we having for dinner?

2. Speak it with more volume and stress:
   What are we having for dinner? What are *we* having for dinner? What are we having for *dinner*?

3. Speak the italicized word with a stress and a downward inflection (\ ).
   What *are* \ we having for dinner?

Deciding which words to emphasize in a text is crucial to bringing out the text's meaning. In normal conversation we do not have a problem with this because we know what we want to say and provide the appropriate emphasis naturally. When we are trying to bring written words to life, we have to determine what the *author* meant to say and to stress. Here are some general guidelines to follow. They must not be used slavishly, because language is flexible.

1. Stress the word in a phrase that carries the meaning forward. For example: "It looks like it's *raining* outside." Here a verb carries the meaning. In the phrase "a *storm* is coming," the noun carries the meaning.

2. Do not stress the prepositions. You would not say "It looks like it's raining *outside*" (unless someone thought it might be raining somewhere else and you want to stress where it is raining).

3 Avoid stressing words that indicate place or time, unless you want to emphasize the place or time something is happening.

4. Seldom should you emphasize adjectives and adverbs. It makes your speech sound melodramatic. For example: "Today I had a *really* big problem"; or "I looked in the shop window and saw a *gorgeous* ring."

5. When something is brought up twice in a passage, emphasize it the first time to introduce it, but not the second time. For example: "Dad, I got my *grades* today. My best grade was *an A!*"

PUTTING IT ALL TOGETHER

I have been discussing six dimensions of oral interpretation. Although looked at in isolation, they all must work together in order for a reading to be sensible and filled with life. It is time now to demonstrate how these techniques are coordinated and employed during the practice and performance of a Scripture reading.

Before the reader can practice combining the use of these techniques, he or she needs to look carefully at the text and determine which skills to employ and where to use them, then find a way to cue himself or herself so that carefully wrought choices unfold as planned. One might simply memorize where the various points of emphasis, inflection, and movement are. A surer approach would be to mark the text with cues that remind the reader where to increase pace and energy, how to stress a phrase, where to pause, and so forth.

You may have heard it said that you should not write in books. Somewhere early in my career as a student I learned how wrong that is. Have you ever tried to buy a textbook for a class that someone else had already underlined? It helps, doesn't it? Today, except for the fiction I buy for leisure reading, I do not own a book I have read that is not marked with marginal comments, underscoring, and highlighting. (It would be a disappointment to this author if he were to see that this copy of your lector training book was not filled with marks and notations already.) Marking your text is a *good* thing to do. Especially if you are going to use it for performing. Ask your church choir director to show you some samples of music the choir has performed. The director's copy will be filled with strong, clear, often colorful markings to indicate how to phrase the music, where to repeat sections, and when to sing softly or loudly. It might look confusing, but the person who makes the cues in the music knows exactly what he or she means. And the marks prove extremely useful in the moment of performance when the director does not have time to reconsider how things are supposed to go. Many people write in their Bibles to underline or comment on special passages. You are encouraged to do this too, but for a different reason. You need to have a performance text that is filled with cues to guide your live presentation. You might want to make a photocopy of your text or use a computer Bible program to print it out. This way you can make the print large and easy to see. If you use a loose page with the text printed on it, place it in a Bible during your performance. I spoke earlier about the negative symbolic effect of using what appears to be disposable Scripture. If your church uses a large-print Bible or lectionary kept on the lectern, you should think twice about marking it up. If you do, use light, erasable pencil markings.

How do you key your text for performance? That will be up to you. You may use colored pens for underlining or highlighting. You might invent symbols to cue you. (As a singer, I use a small check mark to indicate the places where I am to breathe.) You might write things in the margins to guide your presentation. Discuss with people in your group the various symbols and markings that work for them. Then experiment and settle on what works for you. Remember to make clear markings but to keep your text neat and readable.

The passage that follows has been keyed according to the manner used in this chapter. (These marks are merely examples. In your own work you can use colors and symbols to guide you.) As a reminder, these are the cues and their meanings as they are used in this book:

One line (|) is a pause. Two lines (| |) indicate a long pause. A rising inflection is an upward slash (/). A falling inflection is a downward slash (\ ). *Italics* indicate a word or phrase to be emphasized with stress and/or volume. When a phrase is to be delivered with audience eye contact, it is <u>underlined.</u> If the reader is to look up and away to cast a thought or image for consideration by the audience, the phrase is in **bold print**.

Your purpose here will be to study the markings in the passage and prepare to read it publicly. If you are in a small group, take turns reading the passage for one another and offering feedback.

Then Jesus said to the disciples, | | "There was a rich man who had a *manager*, | and *charges* were brought to him that this man was *squandering* his property. | | So he *summoned* him | and said to him, '/ What *is* this that I hear about you \ ? | | Give me an *accounting* of your management, | because you can*not* be my manager any longer.' | | Then the manager said to *himself*, | | '/ What will I do, *now* \ that my master is taking the position away from me? | | I am not strong enough to *dig* /, and I am ashamed to *beg* \. | | \ **I have *decided* what to do** / | so that, when I am dismissed as manager, people may *welcome* me into their *homes*.' | | So /, summoning his master's *debtors* one by one /, | | he asked the first, 'How much do *you* owe my master \?' | | He answered, 'A hundred jugs of *olive oil* \.' | | [The manager] said to him, | | '/ *Take* your bill \, | | sit down quickly, and make it *fifty*.' | | Then he asked another, | 'And how much do *you* owe /?' | | He replied, 'A hundred containers of *wheat* \.' | | He said to him, 'Take *your* bill and make it *eighty*.' | | And his master *commended* the dishonest manager because he had acted shrewdly; | | for the children of this age are / *more shrewd* \ in dealing with their own generation than are the / *children of light* \. | | And I tell you, | make friends for / *yourselves* \ by means of dishonest wealth | so that when it is gone, they may welcome *you* into the eternal homes." (Luke 16:1-9)

Now, as a final exercise, select a passage and prepare it for presentation to the group. This is your final project before completing your basic training as a lector. Remember to do your Bible study so that you can be confident of the text's meaning. If appropriate, provide a brief introduction to the lesson. Remember also to use what you have learned about posture, breath control, and voice as you perform your reading before others. After each person has presented his or her reading, offer feedback as usual. Also, be sure to celebrate the learning that each has achieved in working toward the goal of being an effective lay reader of Scripture.

COMMISSIONING

The assumption is that if you have read this far and worked on the exercises provided in this book, you will have gained a number of useful skills relating to serving as a lector. You may have worked with a training group and gained additional assistance from an instructor and from the kind critique of your peers. It is also presumed that by now you have considered carefully whether or not to undertake this ministry. Maybe you, like Janet in chapter 1, are still wondering if this is for you. If so, please continue to pray about it as you discern whether you have the spiritual gifts and the time and energy to do this well. If you do accept this call to serve your congregation as a messenger of God's Word, then a word of commissioning is in order. Perhaps your congregation will want to celebrate with you and your group by having a brief order of installation during a worship service. Regardless, let me offer you this final word. It comes from the one with whom the introduction of this work began, Martin Luther: "The Holy Scriptures require a humble reader who shows reverence and fear toward the Word of God and constantly says, 'Teach me, teach me, teach me!' " (*Table Talk*). May you be such a reader and serve the church with humility, reverence, and understanding. Amen.

Appendixes

APPENDIX A
CREATIVE APPROACHES TO
SCRIPTURE READING

In addition to the traditional way of reading Scripture in worship, there are several creative and effective means that can be employed. They might be reserved for special occasions such as celebrations on the Day of Pentecost or Easter. Or they might be used more frequently by congregations that have gifted people who are willing to share their talents in the ongoing ministry of proclamation. The effective reading of Scripture always requires rehearsal. If any of the following approaches are used, be sure to plan for ample practice time to coordinate the efforts of all participants.

MIME AND DANCE

If you have mimes or dancers in your congregation, recruit them to perform while a text is read. This might be especially appropriate when Bible stories are being read. It would be difficult to choreograph a list of laws from the book of Leviticus or a theological argument from the letters of Paul. But Old Testament narratives or Gospel parables might well lend themselves to the movement and drama that mime and dance can portray. You might also recruit some musicians to provide a fitting musical score to accompany the reading and the movement.

SIGNING

The use of signing might be a regular part of a congregation's worship if there is a significant population of hearing-impaired persons present. But those without hearing challenges can also appreciate signing as a form of dance. The physical movement of a graceful signer can add a layer of symbolism to a reading and have a powerful effect on those who watch and listen.

MUSICAL AND VISUAL ELEMENTS

As suggested above, appropriately selected and tastefully played music can make a fitting accompaniment for a reading. The texture of the music should match the mood of the text, and the instrumentation should not be overpowering. The focus should remain on the word. One tasteful combination of instruments that is available in many congregations is flute with piano or guitar accompaniment. But other combinations can work just as well. Consider your local talent pool. This might be a good way to involve talented young people in worship.

Visual accompaniment for readings can be achieved through slide presentations or digital images projected on a screen. Here, too, the focus is on the word. Select images that do not dominate the imagination. The capacity to darken the room is helpful when screen projection is used in worship.

HYMNS AND ANTHEMS

If a worship service is designed to include many lessons, the readings might be interspersed with choral or congregational singing. This pattern is found in the "lessons and carols" format frequently used at Christmastime. A similar approach can be used when dealing with especially long readings, like those appointed for Passion Sunday. Many congregations choose to read the narrative in its entirety from one of the Gospels. In Luke, the reading goes from chapters 22 through 23; to read it straight through would take perhaps twenty minutes. In order to provide variety and maintain interest, break the reading into scenes and intersperse them with choral anthems and hymns. This allows for the congregation to participate in the reading and provides people with time for reflection and response. (When this is done, you might suggest to the pastor that a sermon is unnecessary. The text is powerful on its own, and reading it with music will take up most of the service time.)

USE OF THE LITURGICAL CHOIR

Choirs can assist with Scripture readings in a number of useful ways. Two have already been suggested: providing music to underscore a reading and offering anthems that are woven into groups of readings. Another common idea is to allow the choir to present a lesson that has been set to music. This might follow a lector's reading of the text, in which case the anthem stands as a musical commentary on the lesson. At other times it might make sense to allow the choral work to be the only rendering of the text. This works especially well with the psalms.

Perhaps the most overlooked use of the choir is to use the group in a nonmusical way, by providing sound effects for Scripture readings. Here are three examples:

1. Let the choir provide the crowd sounds during a reading of the passion narrative. This is especially effective when Pontius Pilate calls to the crowd and demands that they choose whom to release, Jesus or Barabbas. The text itself will provide clues for the choir's involvement. It tells what the crowd is shouting (for example, "Crucify him!" and "Give us Barabbas!") and it tells

when to crescendo (as in, "but they shouted all the more"). As the voices grow in volume and intensity, the voice of Pilate needs to shout above the people to be heard. This builds tremendous tension and makes the story surge with passion.

2. During a reading of the Pentecost story from Acts 2, use the choir to provide the sound effects as the Holy Spirit enters the picture. Choir members might crumple pieces of paper to suggest the crackling of fire or make a whooshing sound with their mouths to simulate the "mighty wind" quality of the Spirit's movement. When the scene moves out into the street, the choir might provide the babble of people speaking in many languages.

3. If a reading calls for a soft, unearthly sound, the choir can provide it by having each member hum randomly. This might be used to accompany a Good Friday reading about the death of Jesus. This effect is easy to achieve if the director asks each choir member to hum his or her favorite hymn. The random sound occurs as the many tunes mask each other and create a cacophony.

A READING CHOIR

A creative approach for presenting dramatic Bible stories is to use a reading choir (also known as reader's theater). This is a nonmusical group of voices organized to read in cooperation with one another. The result is that the Bible text unfolds much like a play. If there are several characters that speak in the story, let their lines be assigned to different readers. One person should read the narrator's part.

The reading choir works best when one person serves as the director. The director's job is to determine how the text should be interpreted, divide the reading into character parts, and guide the choir through its rehearsal by making performance sugges-tions. In assigning lines and organizing the material, eliminate from the text those verbal quotation marks that explain who is speaking (such as "then Jesus replied"). These are unnecessary when each character is represented by a different person. Eliminating the verbal quotation marks gives the reading a nat-ural, conversational quality.

RECITAL OF SCRIPTURE

Readers who have a good memory and strong theatrical skills might occasionally choose to recite a biblical text. This works for stories as well as other kinds of material. For example, a reader might assume the persona of Paul and deliver an epistle text as if personally addressing Paul's audience. It would make sense in such a recital for the reader to step out from behind the lectern and make use of an open space in which he or she could move freely to embody the message.

Earlier it was suggested that hand gestures should be used spar-ingly during Scripture readings. This is not the case in reciting memorized Scripture. Here the presenter is "acting out" the work by taking on the persona of the author. Lack of gesture and movement, in this case, would seem wooden and inappropriate. As a beginning strategy, a reader might select a brief parable from the Gospels to memorize and recite before the lector training group. As with all other exercises, the group can provide useful feedback to the lector who wishes to add this style of presenta-tion to his or her repertoire of skills.

APPENDIX B
ANNOTATED BIBLIOGRAPHY

BIBLE COMMENTARIES

There are countless versions of Bible commentaries. The following are familiar resources that are commonly available.

Augsburg Commentary on the Old and New Testaments, Augsburg Fortress, various publication dates
   This is a series of Bible commentaries that, in various volumes, covers all the books of the Bible. It is intended for use by laypeople as well as pastors. Each commentary works through one or two books of the Bible, section by section, offering background information, exegetical insight, and theological reflection.

Interpretation: A Bible Commentary for Teaching and Preaching, John Knox Press, various publication dates
   This series of Bible commentaries features textual reflections by well-known Bible scholars and preachers. It is designed to provide preachers and students with a resource that integrates exegetical research and theological interpretation. The volumes in this series are written in nontechnical, readable prose that will be useful to layreaders.

The Interpreter's Bible, Abingdon Press, first published in 1952
   This collection of twelve volumes is an excellent resource for the layreader. For each book of the Bible it provides background information, including date, authorship, theological perspective, and so forth. It also provides the Revised Standard Version and the King James Version of the Bible

placed in parallel fashion for easy comparison. Next, it offers a verse-by-verse exegetical commentary and includes a preaching commentary for pastoral consideration.

The New Interpreter's Bible, Abingdon Press, published 1995 to present

Like its predecessor collection, this edition of the *Interpreter's Bible* is filled with useful material. The differences are that (1) it is a completely updated work, (2) the parallel Bible translations included are the New International Version and the New Revised Standard Version, and (3) the pastoral commentary is presented as "Reflections," which are less like sermons and more useful as interpretive pointers.

BIBLE DICTIONARIES

The Anchor Bible Dictionary, Bantam Doubleday Dell Publishers, 1992

This six-volume set of books is a comprehensive encyclopedia designed for serious biblical scholarship. It provides a particularly clear view of the world of the ancient Near East and the Mediterranean basin. It would be useful for lectors who wish to dig deeply into the background of the material they read.

Eerdmans Dictionary of the Bible, William B. Eerdmans Publishing Company, 2000

This 1,500-page, single-volume dictionary is written for scholars and students of the Bible. It provides brief articles on 5,000 subjects and contains dozens of illustrations and color maps. Though technical, it is also readable and useful for the layperson seeking to learn about biblical characters, places, and terms.

The Interpreter's Dictionary of the Bible, Abingdon Press, first published in 1962

This resource describes itself as "an illustrated encyclopedia" of the Bible. It is in five large volumes and provides detailed articles on countless biblical topics. This reference collection is designed for use by pastors and theologians as well as "anyone who would read the Bible with intelligence."

BOOKS ON ORAL INTERPRETATION OF SCRIPTURE

Effective Speech Communication in Leading Worship, by Charles L. Bartow, Abingdon Press, 1988

This book, as the author says in the introduction, is "for anyone, seminary student, pastor, or layperson," interested in worship leadership. It covers many subjects relating to communication in worship, but devotes several chapters to the techniques relating to oral interpretation of Scripture. The author provides clear, detailed instruction in the art of oral interpretation and gives helpful exercises to engage the reader in private practice. For the layreader who seeks an advanced look at the techniques of oral interpretation, this book is worth reading carefully.

Getting the Word Across: Speech Communication for Pastors and Lay Leaders, G. Robert Jacks, William B. Eerdmans Publishing Company, 1995

In this book, Jacks provides a refreshingly nonacademic approach to the topic. He writes in a charming, colloquial style that puts the reader at ease. The book contains humorous anecdotes and illustrations, along with plenty of solid technical material and useful exercises. This is another resource for the lector who wants to explore the techniques of oral interpretation more fully.

How to Read the Bible Aloud: Oral Interpretation of Scripture, Jack C. Rang, Paulist Press, 1994

This book, the author boldly claims in the preface, "was written for you." He is correct, for he is addressing people who have consented to serve as readers of Scripture in worship. In addition to covering the basic topics relating to use of the body and voice and the role of diction in oral interpretation, Rang addresses subjects having to do with literary style of biblical material. The bulk of the book is devoted to teaching the reader how to deal with the particular issues that relate to the oral interpretation of Old and New Testament narratives, the Epistles, and apocalyptic material.

Performing the Word: Preaching as Theatre, Jana Childers, Abingdon Press, 1998

Although written primarily for preachers and about preaching, the author deals with the subject of Scripture reading in a chapter called "Performing the Text." The value of this book for layreaders is to learn from this experienced preacher and actor about the close kinship of proclamation and drama.

Workbook for Lectors and Gospel Readers, Susan E. Myers, Liturgy Training Resources, 2000

For readers using the Revised Common Lectionary, this is a helpful resource. Note that the particular volume listed above is merely an example of the books available in this series. A new volume with relevant texts is printed each year. All appointed readings for the year are provided (in the Revised New American Bible translation), along with three layers of reading helps. First, the lessons themselves are premarked for emphasis (for example, "The man went *away* and began to *publicize* the whole *matter*"). Second, there is an exegetical commentary for each lesson printed at the bottom of the page. Third, there are marginal comments printed alongside the text providing interpretive suggestions. Care should be taken in the use of this resource because the premarked text may not always match the emphasis choices that the lector wishes to make. Also, the attached commentary is abbreviated and may not provide the lector with enough information to guide his or her interpretation of a text. This resource is intended by the publishers to be a workbook for readers and not a performance copy of the texts.

AUDIO AND VIDEO RESOURCES

Ink into Blood, produced by Seraphim Productions and the Sierra Pacific Synod of the Evangelical Lutheran Church in America, 2001
    This videotape resource features an introduction by author Walt Wangerin and the on-screen teaching of Professor Tom Rogers, as well as useful examples given by trained layreaders. Like this book, *Ink into Blood* was designed to be used by groups of people in congregations who are committed to classroom instruction and discussion as they become trained in the techniques of oral interpretation of Scripture.

Lector Training Program and *Proclaiming the Word: Formation for the Reader,* Liturgy Training Resources
    The first resource mentioned above is an audiocassette series that provides basic instruction for lector training. The second is a videotape resource in two parts. Part 1 deals with issues of faith formation for layreaders, and part 2 with the work of the reader. Expert demonstration and commentary by lectors is provided. This publisher also has available in its catalog numerous other written and audio/video resources for the training of layreaders.

OTHER RESOURCES MENTIONED IN THIS BOOK

Concise Encyclopedia of Preaching, edited by Richard Lischer and William H. Willimon, Westminster John Knox Press, 1995
    It is in this collection of articles that Richard Hays' "Exegesis"

is found. Although the book is intended for use by preachers, there are numerous articles that might be of interest to the lay-reader. They include articles on the Word of God; hermeneutics (interpretation); proclamation; books of the Bible; use of language; drama; communication; and use of voice.

Strong, Loving, and Wise: Presiding in Liturgy, Robert W. Hovda, The Liturgical Press, 1976

This book is written for those who preside over worship, especially Roman Catholic priests. Nonetheless, in addition to the information referred to in chapter 1 of this book, for layreaders there is helpful information that relates to presence and style in worship leadership.